Port Elgin Ontario Book 1 and Area in Colour Photos, Saving Our History One Photo at a Time

Photography
by Barbara Raué
2014

Series Name:
Cruising Ontario

Book 107: Port Elgin Book 1

Cover photo: 543 Mill Street, Port Elgin, see Page 21

Series Name: Cruising Ontario
Saving Our History One Photo at a Time
in colour photos

Other Books by Barbara Raue

Coins of Gold

Arrows, Indians and Love

The Life and Times of Barbara
Volume 1: Inventions That Have Enhanced My Life
Volume 2: Entertainment That I Have Enjoyed
Volume 3: East Coast Trips
Volume 4: Olympics Have Always Intrigued Me
Volume 5: Wonders of the World
Volume 6: Caribbean Cruises We Have Enjoyed
Volume 7: Animals
Volume 8: Storms and Other Major Disasters in My Lifetime
Volume 9: Wars, Terrorist Attacks and Major Disasters

The Cromwell Family Book

Laura Secord Discovered

Daddy Where Are You?

Visit Barbara's website to view all of her books
http://barbararaue.ca

Port Elgin

Originally, the village of Port Elgin was named Normanton. In 1873, the community was named after James Bruce, 8th Earl of Elgin, a former Governor-General of the Province of Canada. In the 1990s, Port Elgin was merged into the town of Saugeen Shores. Port Elgin is close to MacGregor Point Provincial Park and Southampton in Bruce County; the community has several beaches on Lake Huron.

In 1854, Benjamin Shantz acquired a sawmill on Mill Creek from George Butchart. Nearby he built a gristmill and within three years a community of 250 people developed around these mills. Stores, hotels and tanneries were built and a village plot for Port Elgin was laid out in 1857. Businessmen Henry Hilker, Samuel Bricker, and John Stafford contributed to the development of the settlement.

The original economic development of Port Elgin during the 19th century was based on its harbour facilities on Lake Huron constructed in 1857–1858. This made the village a distribution centre for the surrounding agricultural region. The arrival of the Wellington, Grey and Bruce Railway in 1872 further stimulated the growth of the community. The increasing urbanization of Ontario and the increased importance of the road network for transporting goods resulted in a declining economy and population. More recently, recreation and the nearby Bruce Nuclear Generating Station have dominated the local economy.

The Port Elgin and North Shore Railway is a two foot (610 mm) narrow gauge heritage railway. The railway operates excursion trains along the beach on a one-mile route in downtown Port Elgin. The round trip takes about twenty minutes.

Hepworth

Hepworth is located at the base of the Bruce Peninsula, on Highway 6 east of Sauble Beach.

Sauble Beach

Sauble Beach is a resort community on the eastern shore of Lake Huron. The beach is seven miles long.

Shallow Lake

Shallow Lake is located on Highway 6 south and east of Hepworth.

Table of Contents

Port Elgin

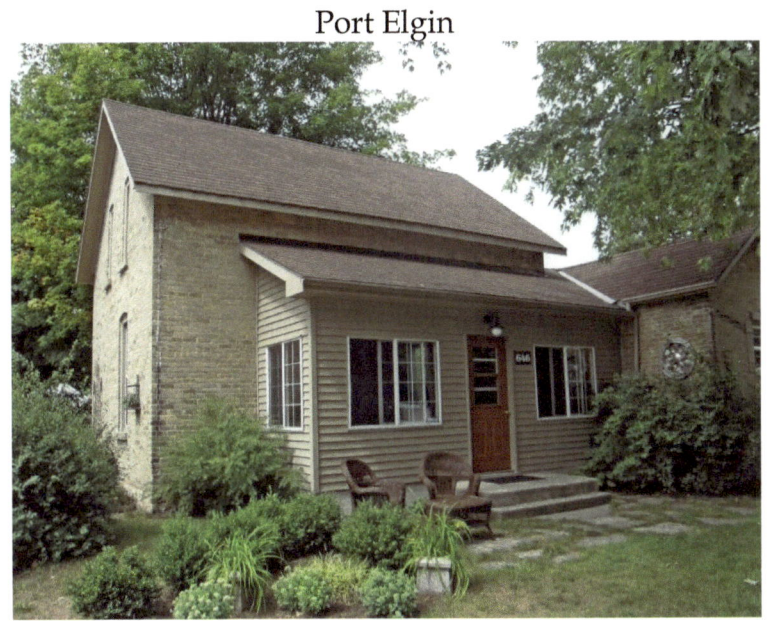

646 Shantz Street - 1½ storey yellow brick – Gothic
Mary and John Zant - 1899

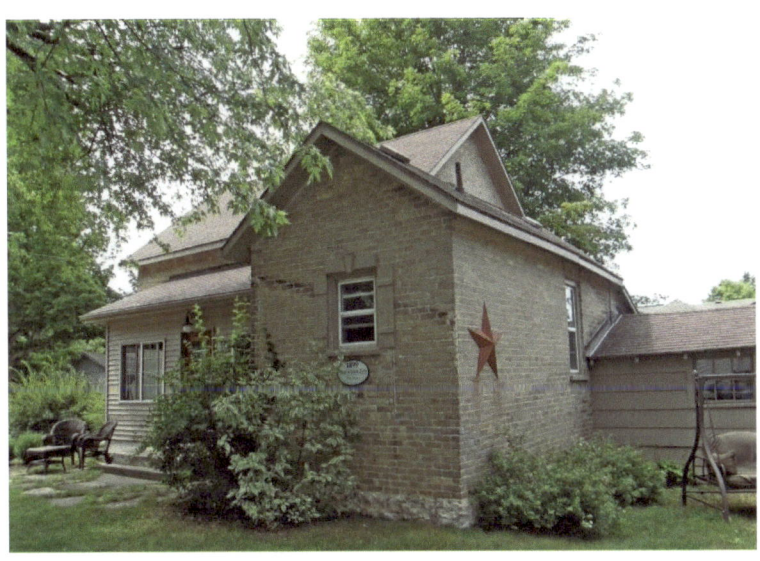

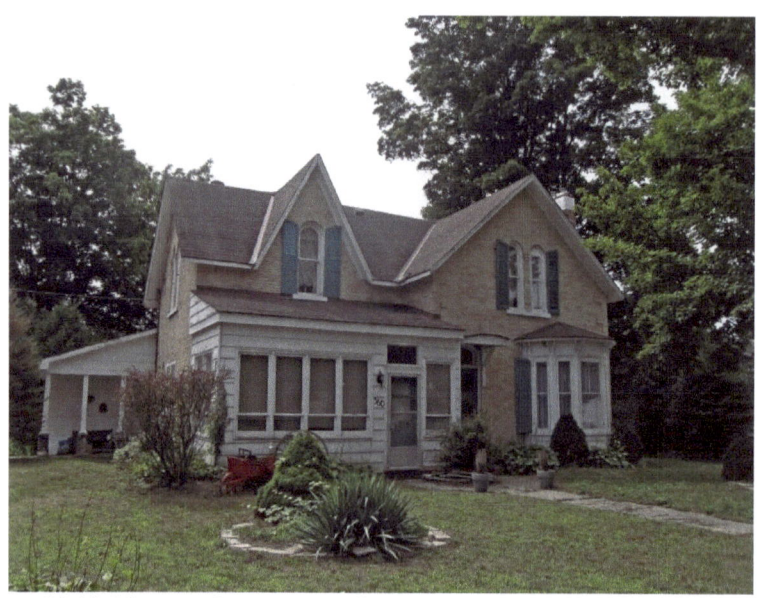

#360 Shantz Street – yellow brick – Gothic Revival

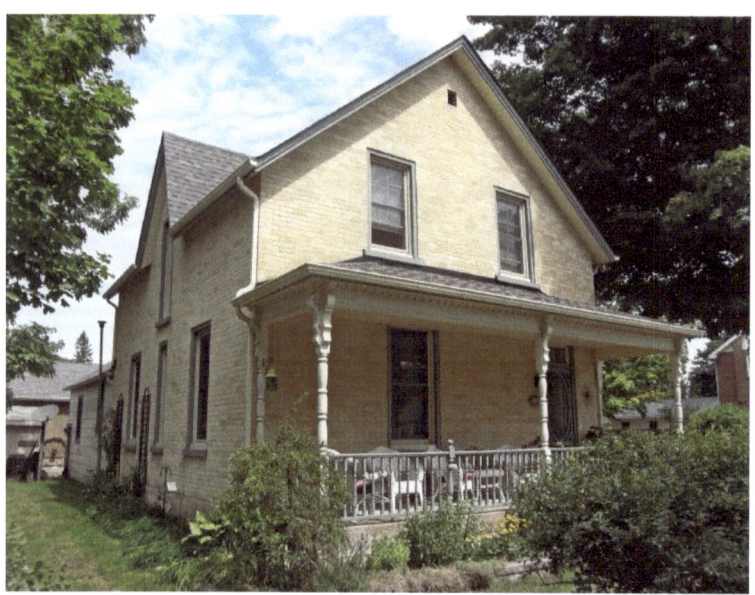

399 Green Street – 1½ storey yellow brick – Gothic style

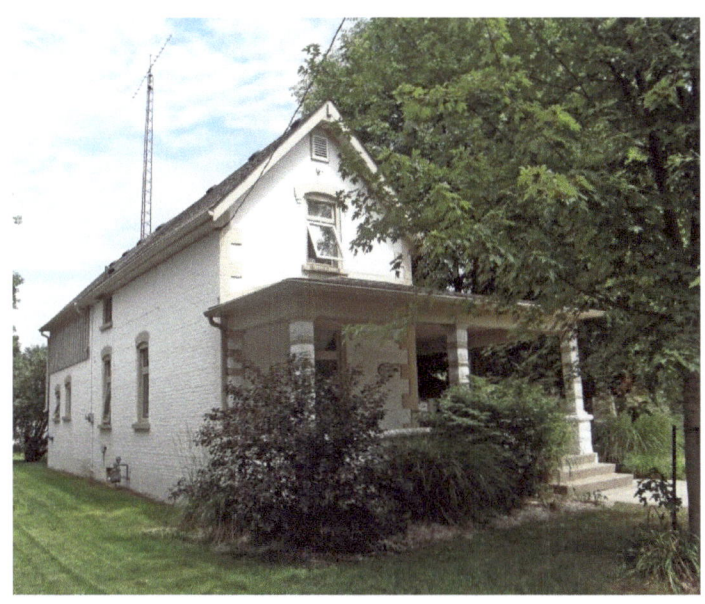

387 Green Street - Harvey J. Gonder, Farm Agent – circa 1895

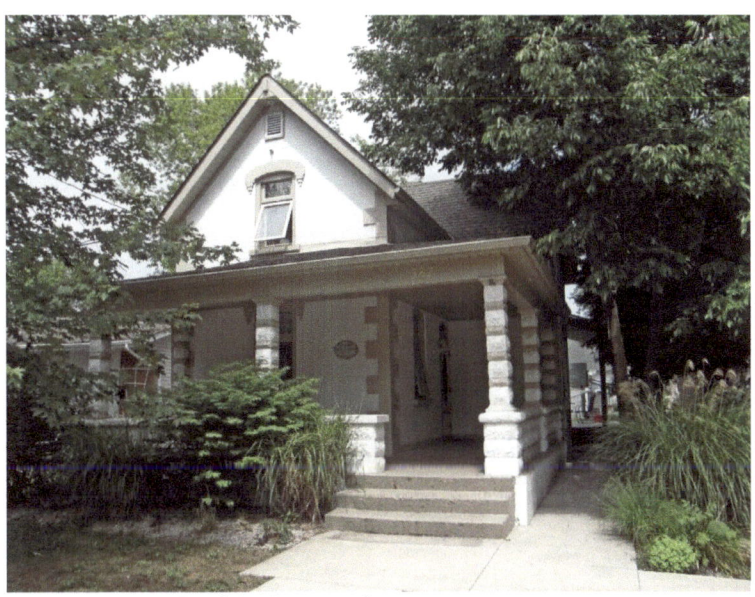

Gothic Revival – corner quoins

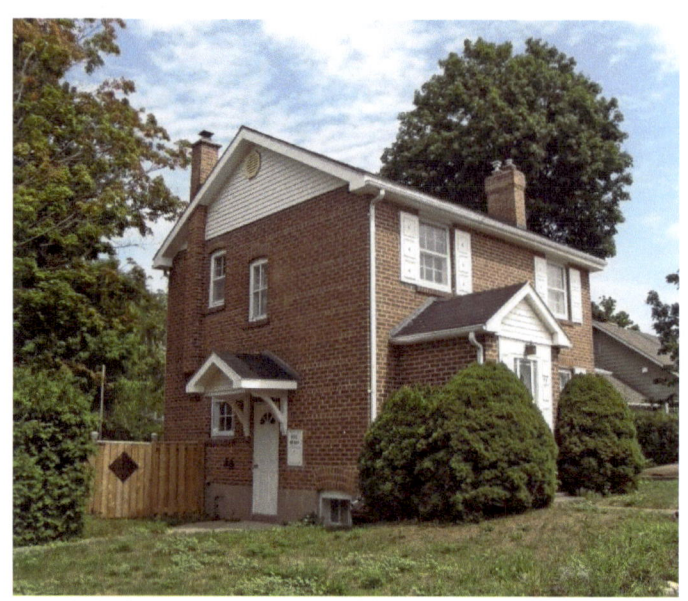

411 Green Street – red brick – two storeys

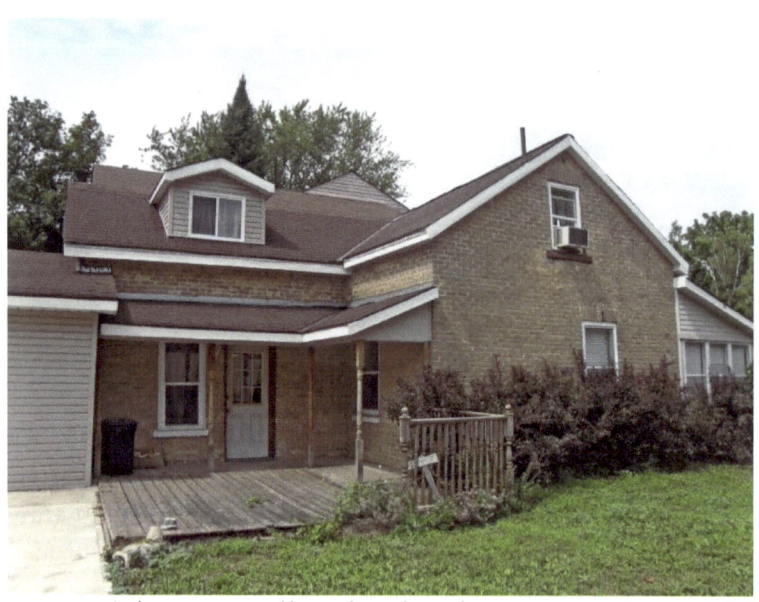

1½ storey yellow brick – dormer in attic

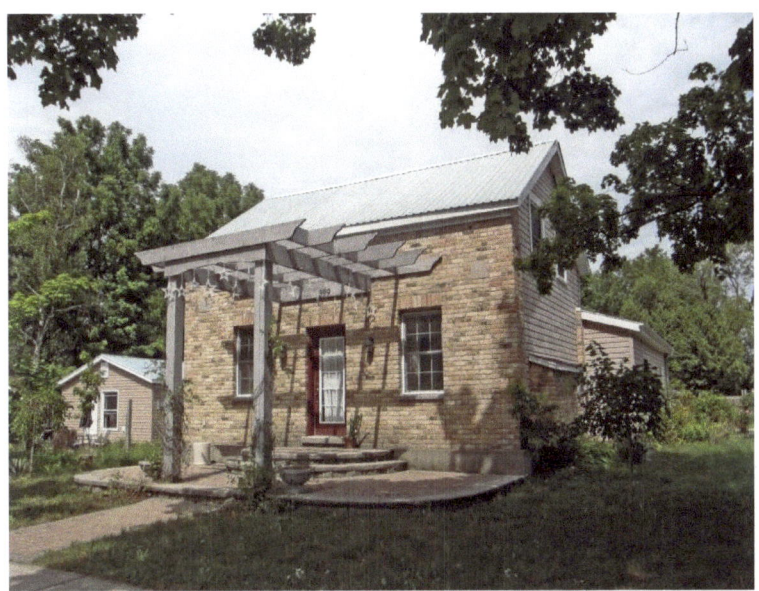

#399 – yellow brick – arbour similar to one Harry built at our townhouse at 100 Quigley Road, Hamilton

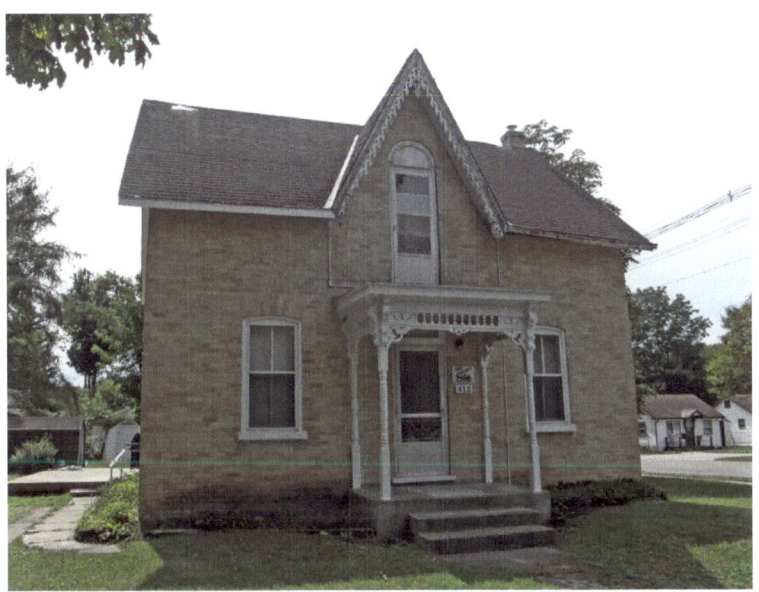

#412 – Gothic Cottage – 1½ storey yellow brick, decorative verge board trim on gable

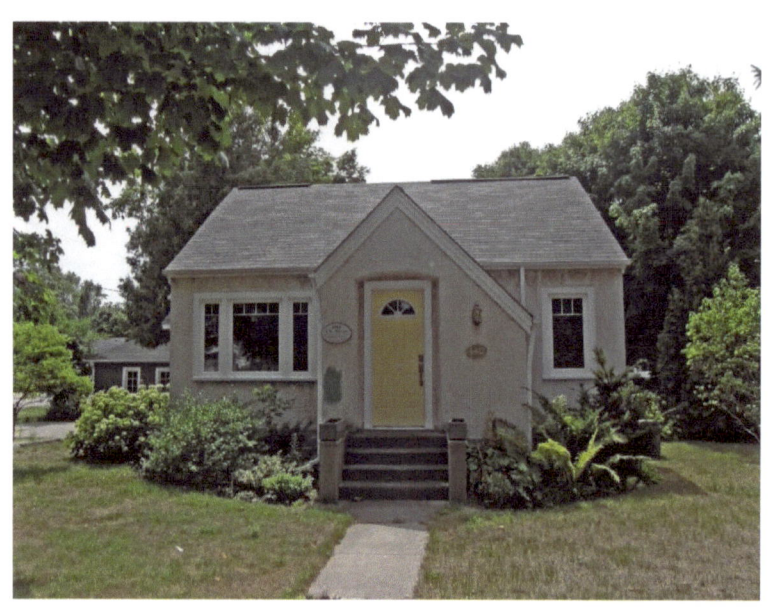

#440 – J. V. Nelles, Medical Doctor – 1945
Stucco exterior

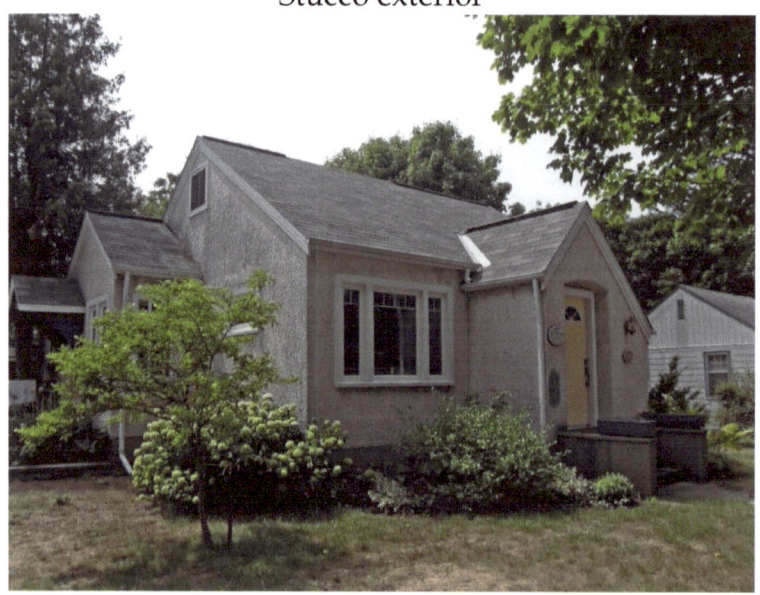

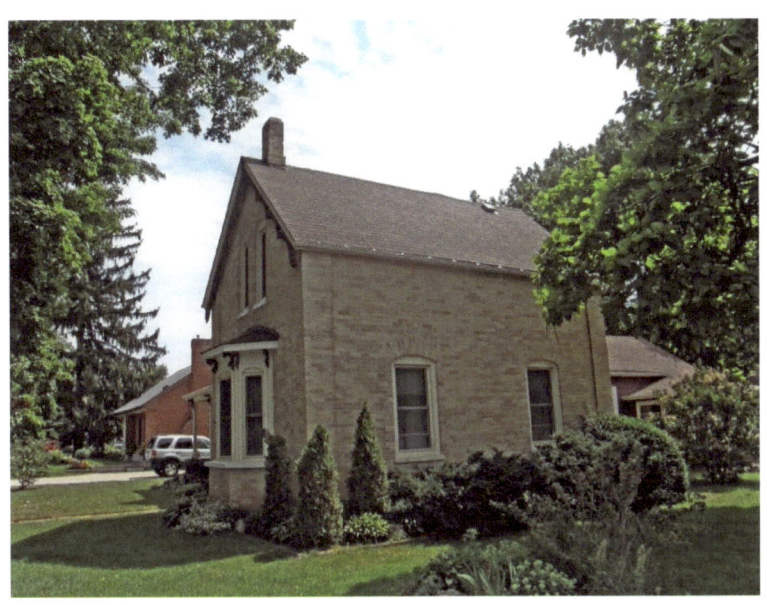

452 Green Street – yellow brick – Gothic Revival
– Verge board trim, bay window

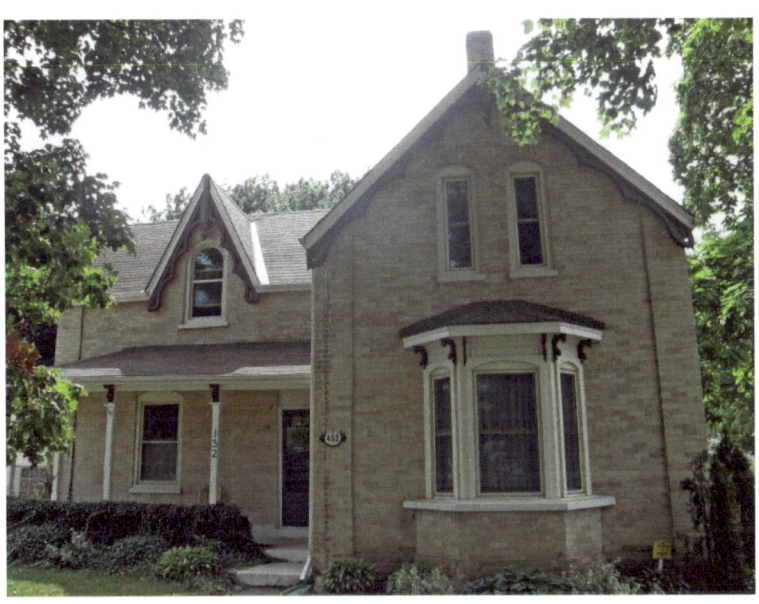

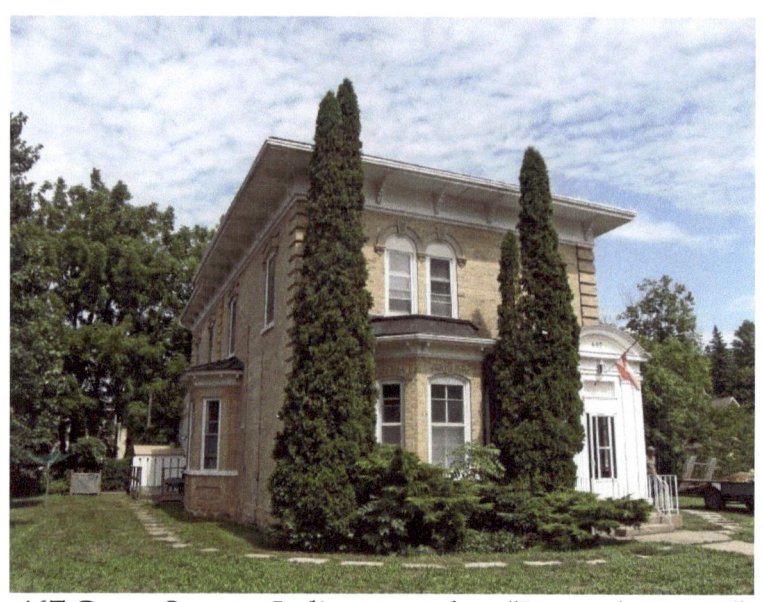

467 Green Street – Italianate style – "Lavrock House"
Single cornice brackets, bay windows

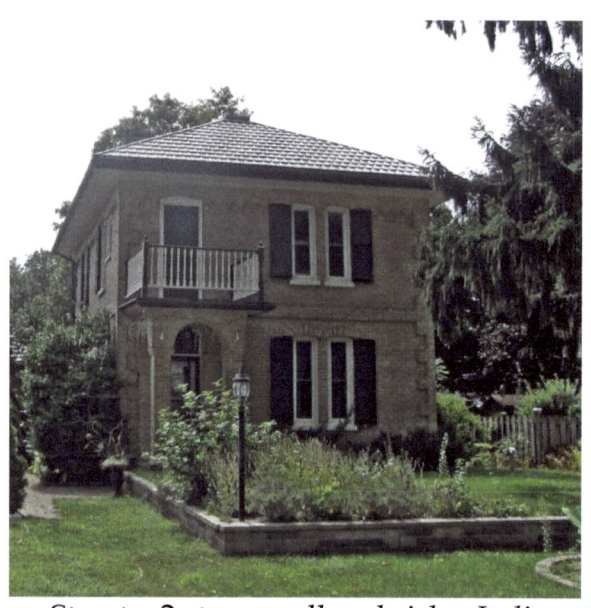

464 Green Street – 2 storey yellow brick – Italianate style,
hipped roof, corner quoins, 2nd floor balcony

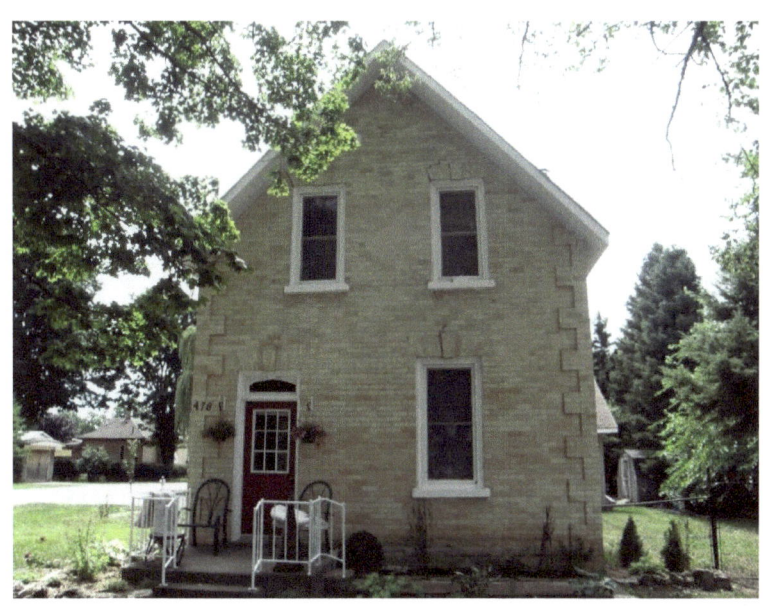

478 Green Street – 1½ storey yellow brick – Gothic Revival
Quoining on corners

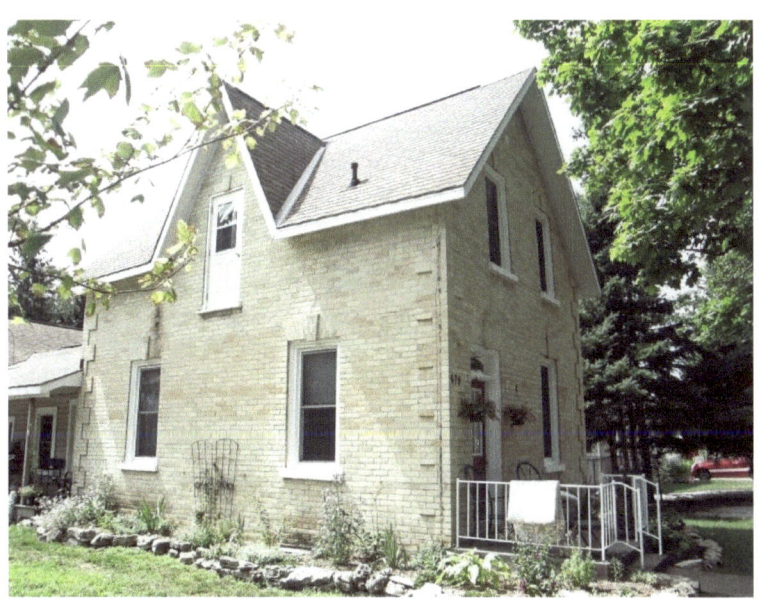

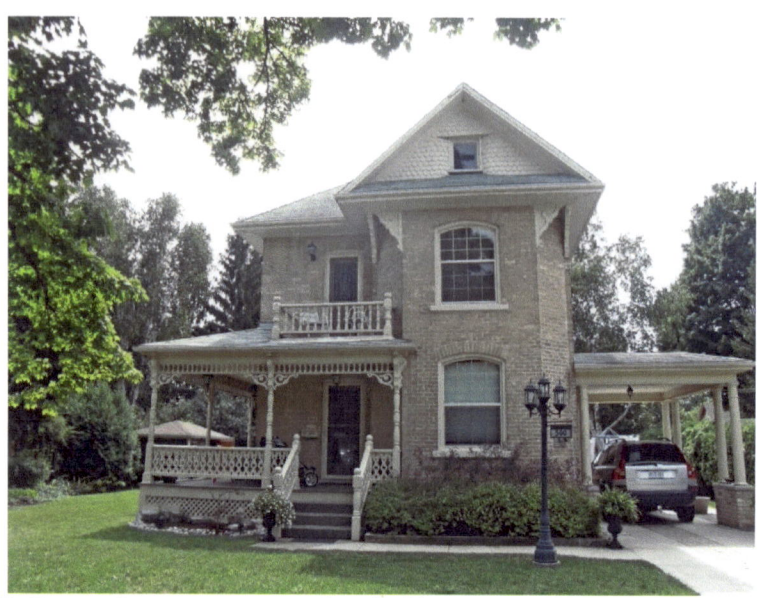

500 Green Street - two-and-a-half storey tower-like bay with projecting eaves and large fretwork pieces resembling brackets, 2nd floor balcony

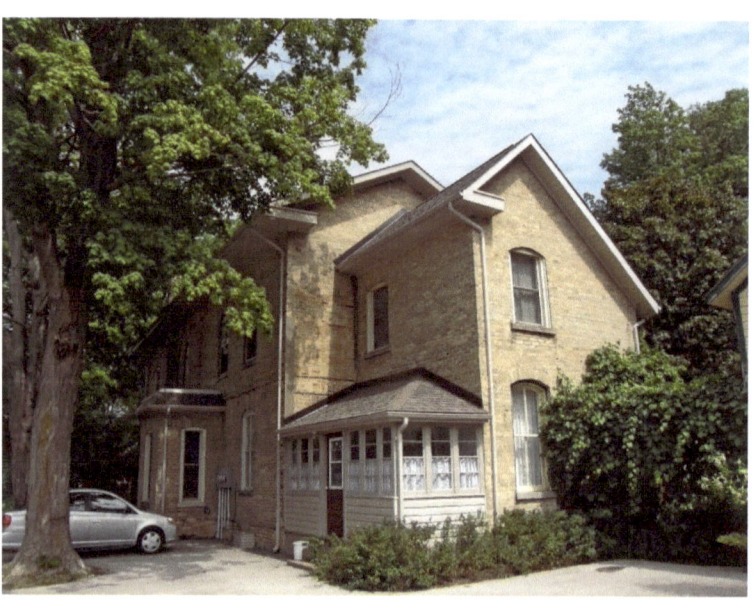

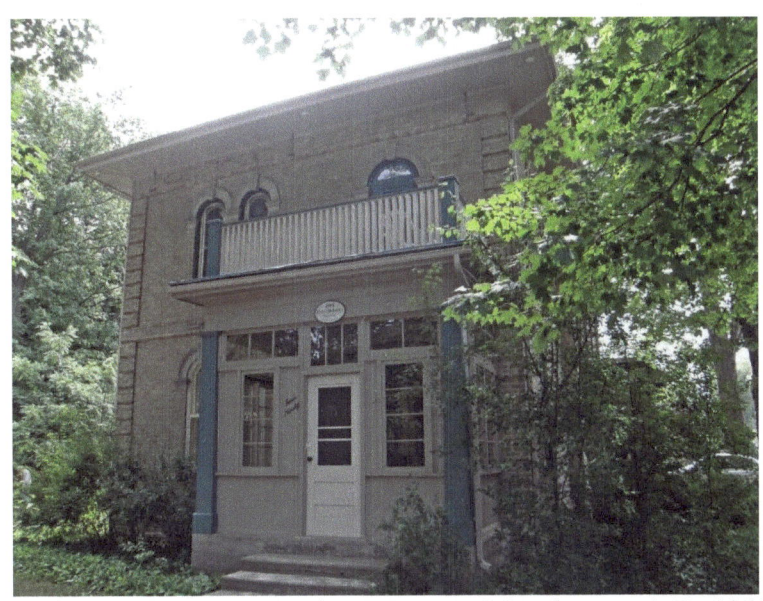

490 Green Street – Hugh McLaren, Merchant - A.D. 1883
2 storey – Italianate style – decorative voussoirs and keystones
above windows

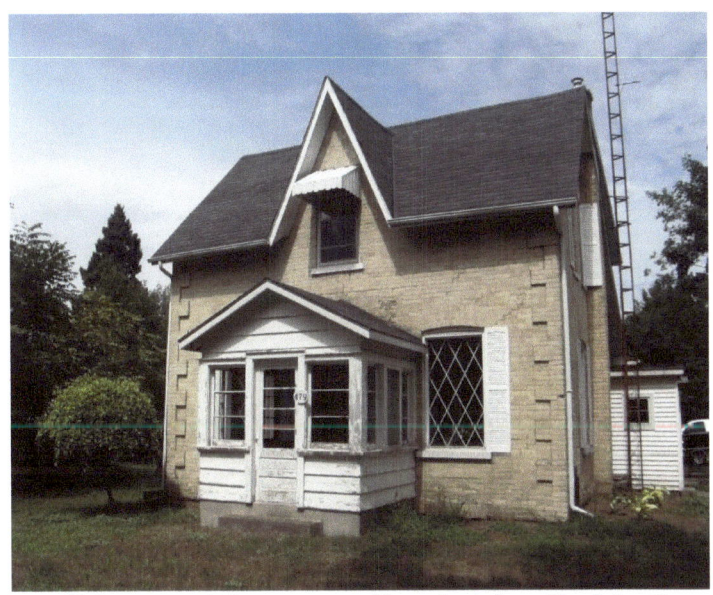

479 Mill Street – 1½ storey yellow brick – Gothic Cottage

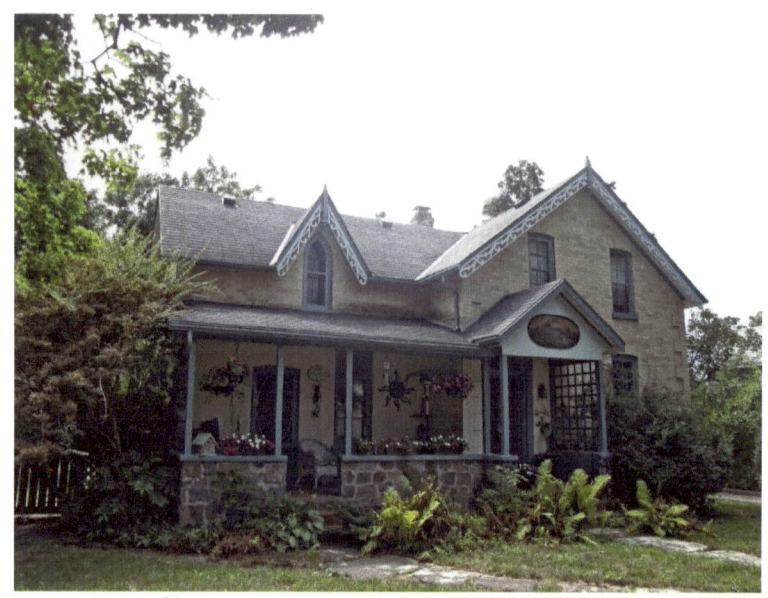

464 Mill Street – Ezra Swartz, Merchant – 1900
Gothic Revival – Verge board trim, cobblestone verandah

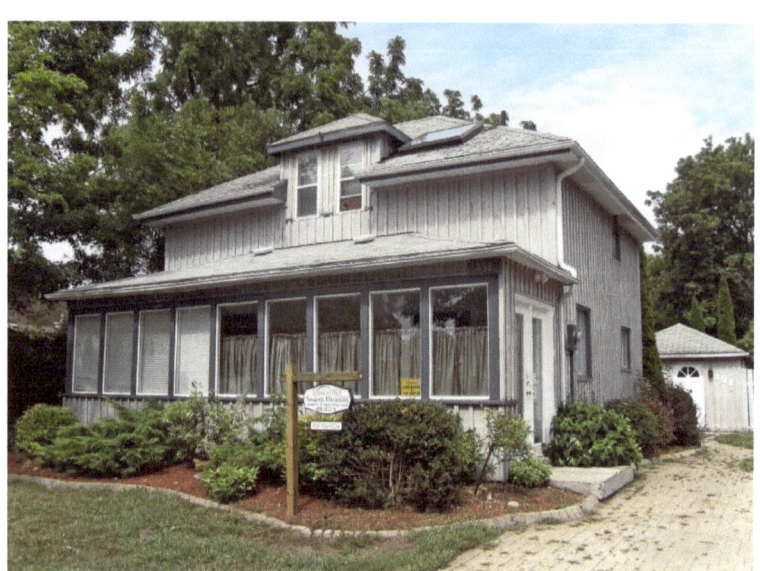

459 Mill Street – Saugeen Hacienda – Italianate style,
dormer in attic

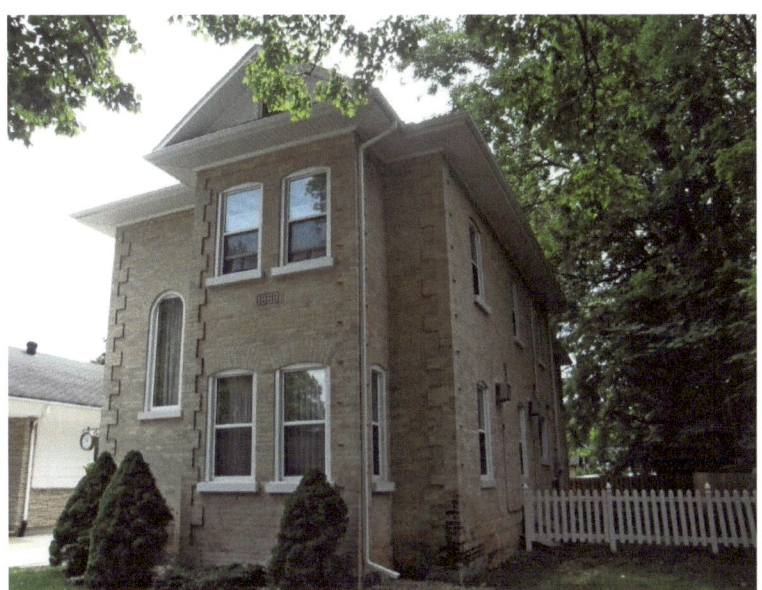

Italianate style – 1888 – yellow brick with two-storey tower
capped by a triangular pediment with window,
Corner quoins

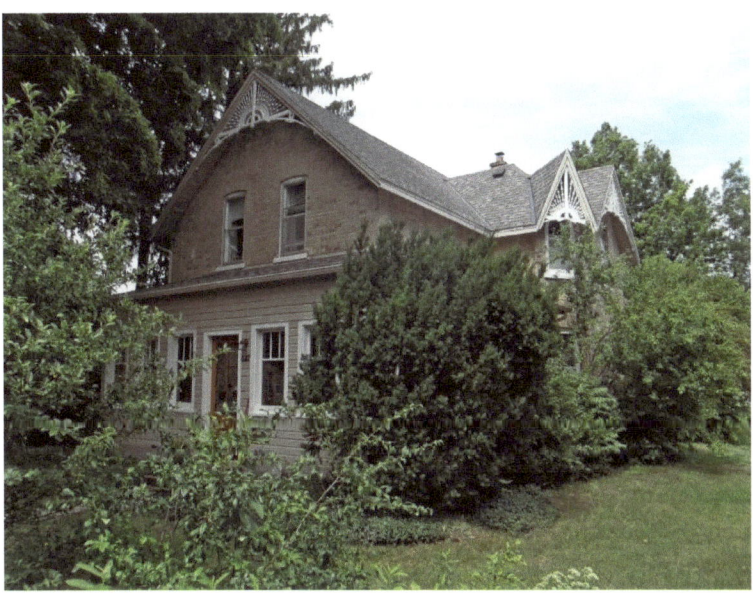

517 Mill Street – yellow brick, Verge board trim, Gothic

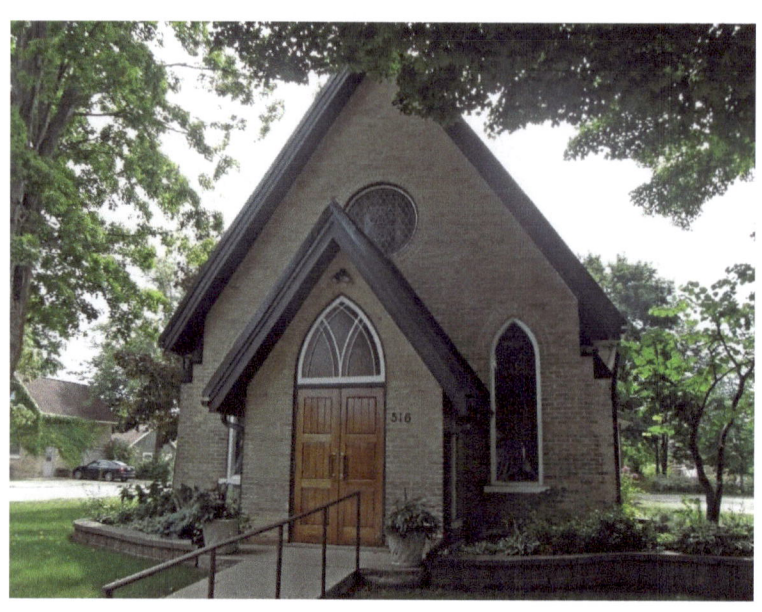

St. John's Anglican Church, 516 Mill Street – rose window, lancet windows

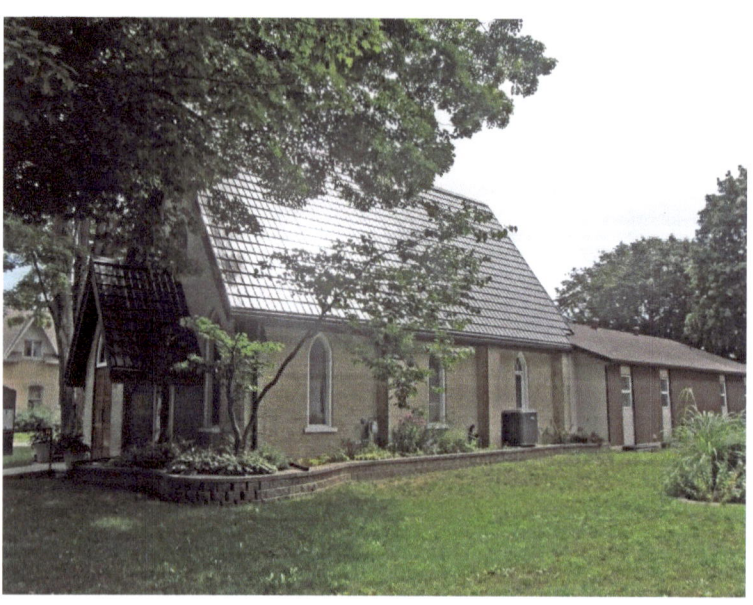

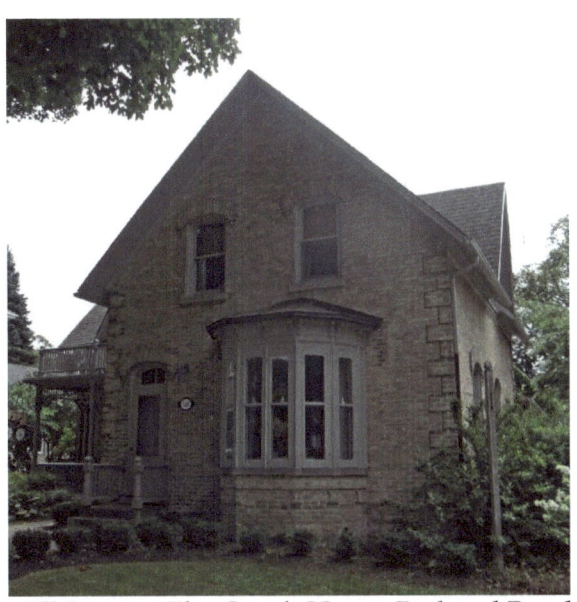

530 Mill Street – The Coach House Bed and Breakfast
Yellow brick, arched voussoirs, cornice brackets on bay window,
quoining on corners

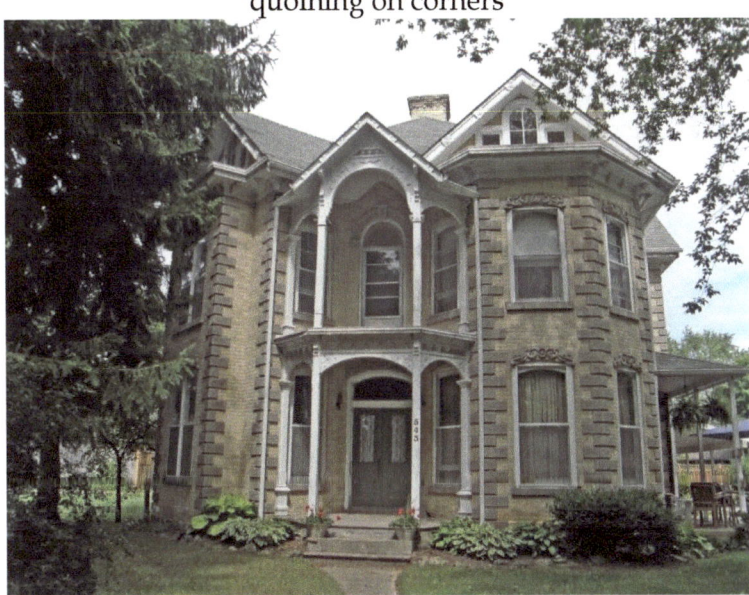

543 Mill Street – Queen Anne style – yellow brick, quoins, Palladian
windows in gables, large fretwork pieces resembling brackets on
eaves of second floor porch, decorative window hoods

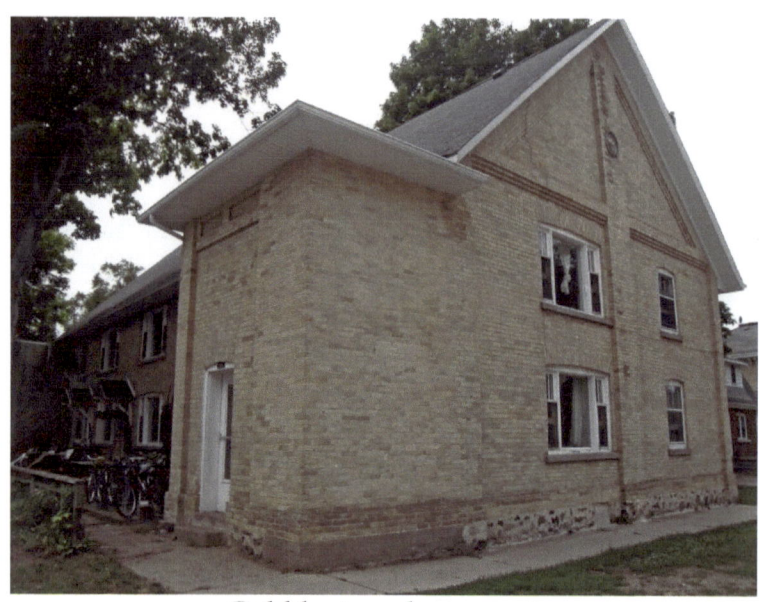

Cobblestone basement
C. M. Church erected A.D. 1871

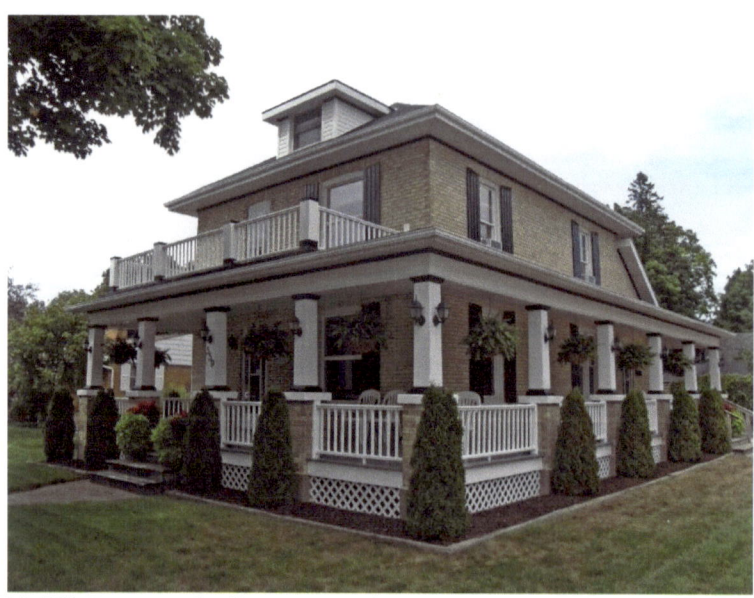

559 Mill Street – Italianate style, wrap-around porch, second
floor balcony, dormer in attic – Henry Ebert, Merchant - 1923

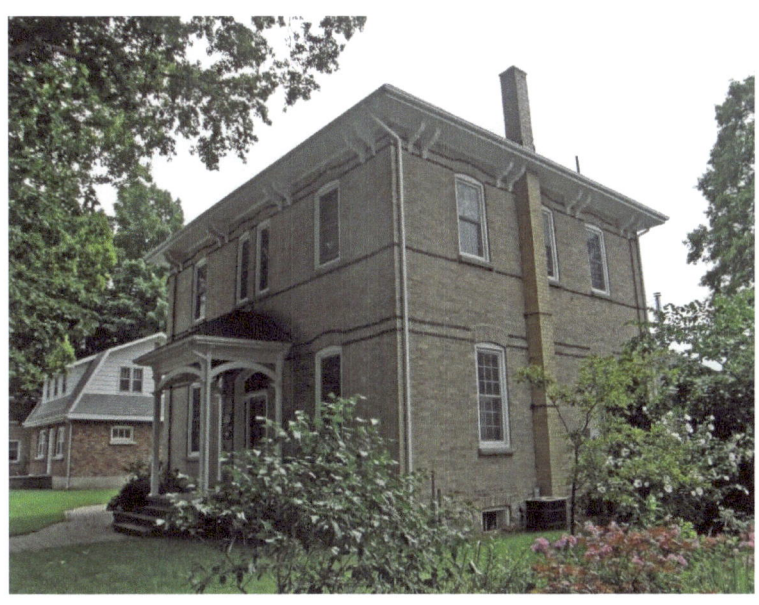

536 Mill Street – yellow brick, Italianate style – paired cornice brackets, dichromatic banding, bay window

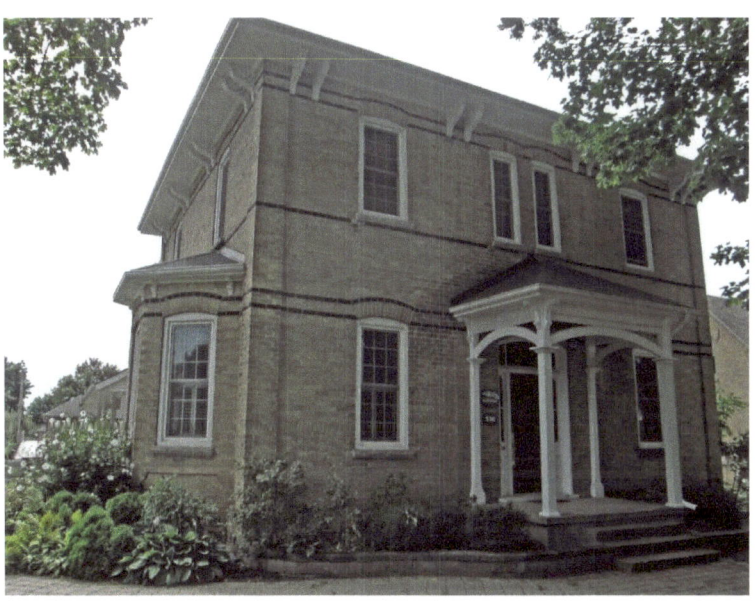

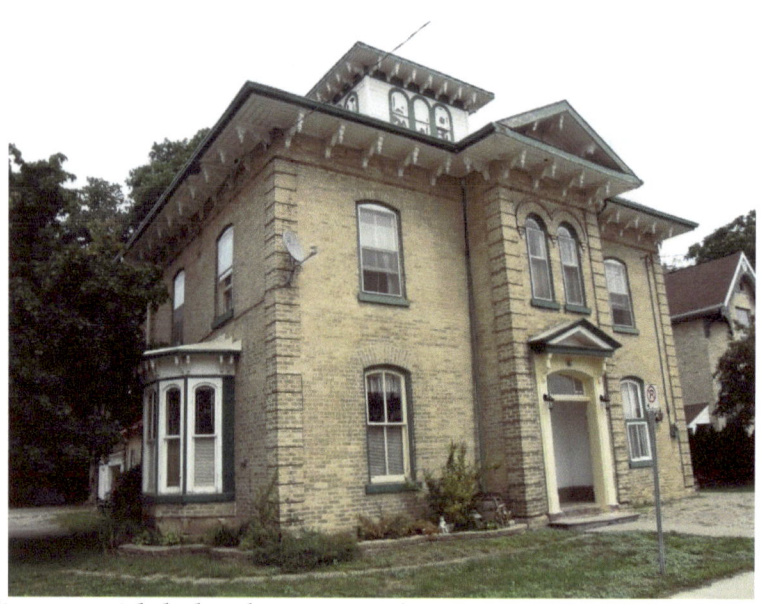

Italianate with belvedere on roof, two storey frontispiece with triangular pediment and arched window hoods, single cornice brackets, bay window on side

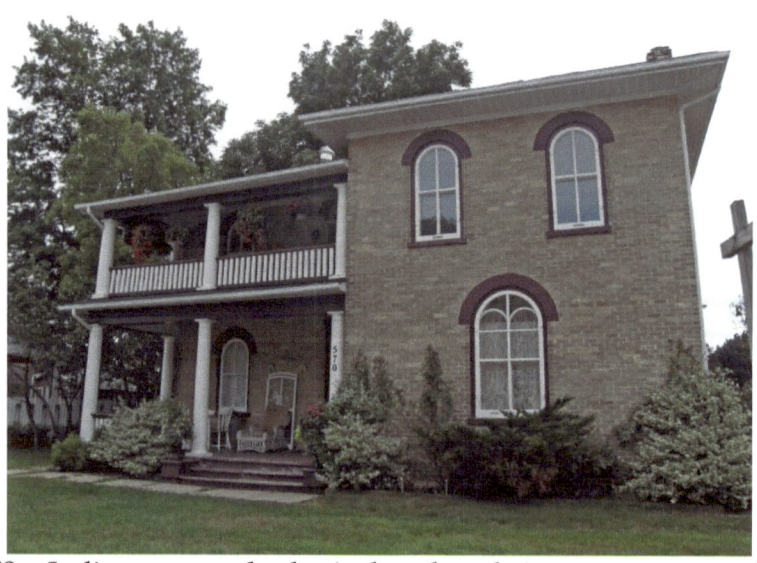

#570 – Italianate – arched window hoods in contrasting colour to yellow brick, 2nd floor verandah

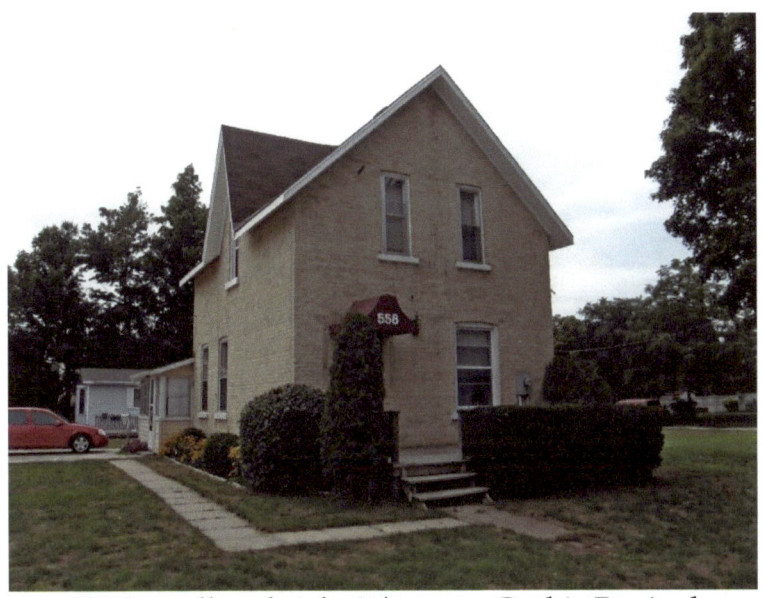

#558 – yellow brick, 1½ storey Gothic Revival

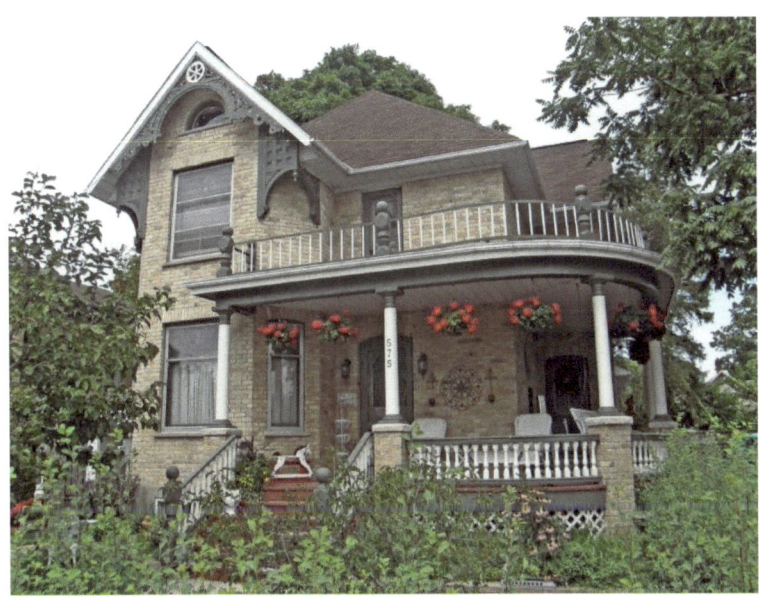

#575 – Italianate style with two-and-a-half storey tower-like bay with projecting eaves and large fretwork pieces resembling brackets, wrap-around verandah on first and second storeys

Downtown

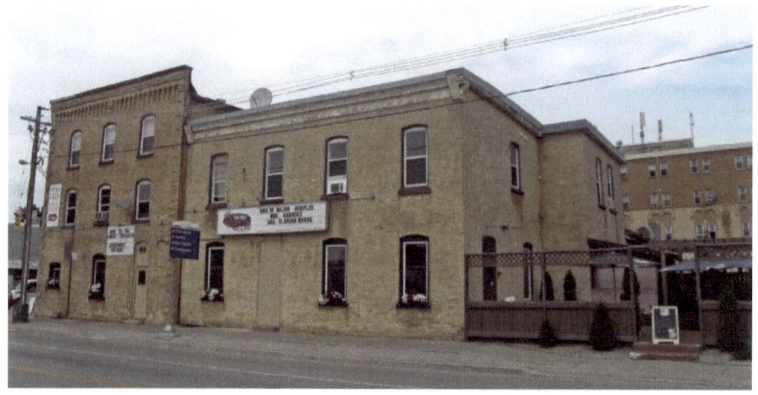

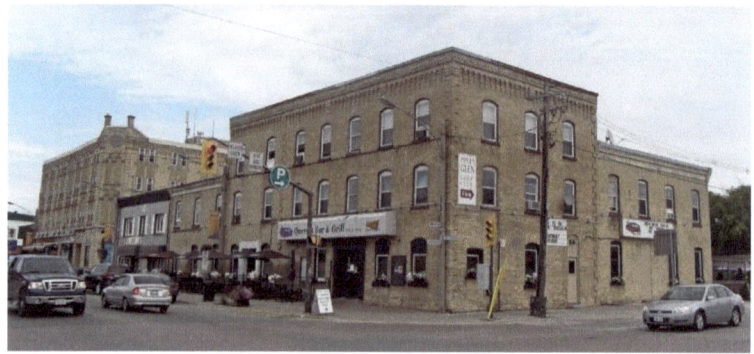

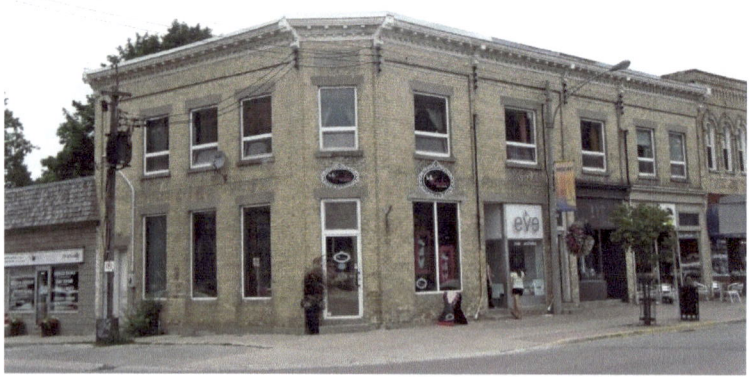

Dentil moulding below cornice brackets

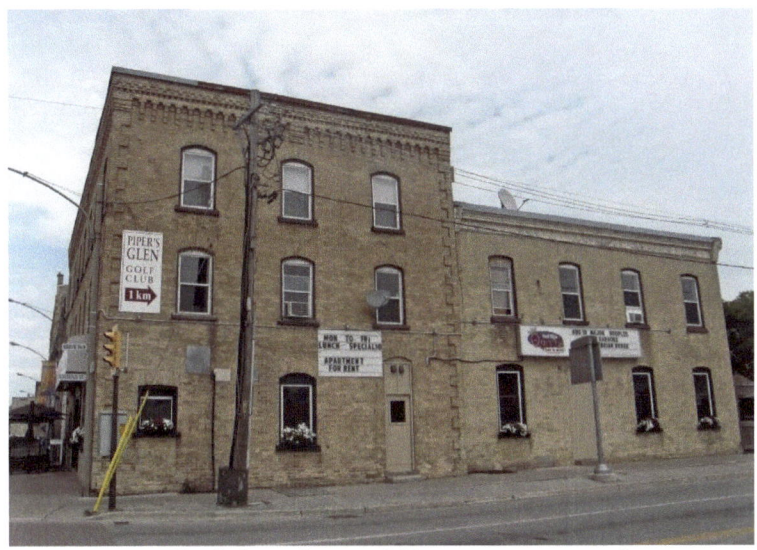

Bevelled dentil moulding, corner quoins

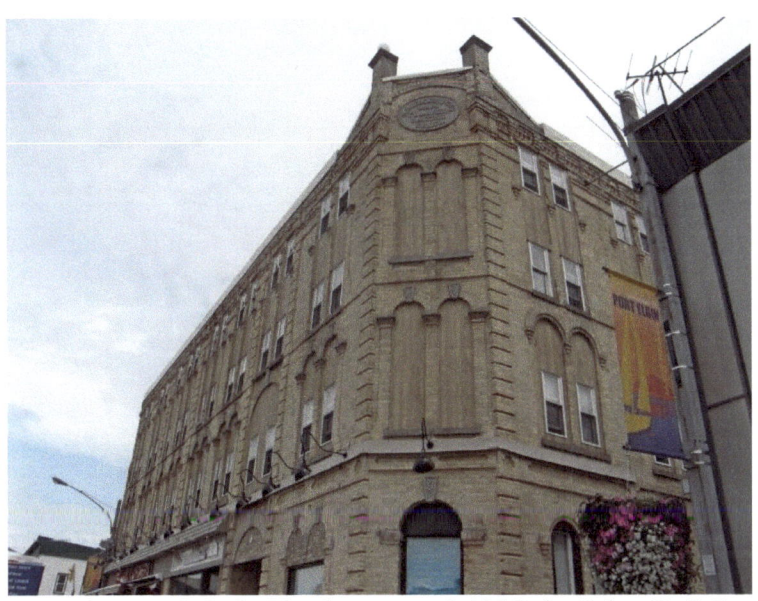

D. O. Bricker and Co's Block, erected 1880, builder D. J. Izzerd,
Arched voussoirs with keystones

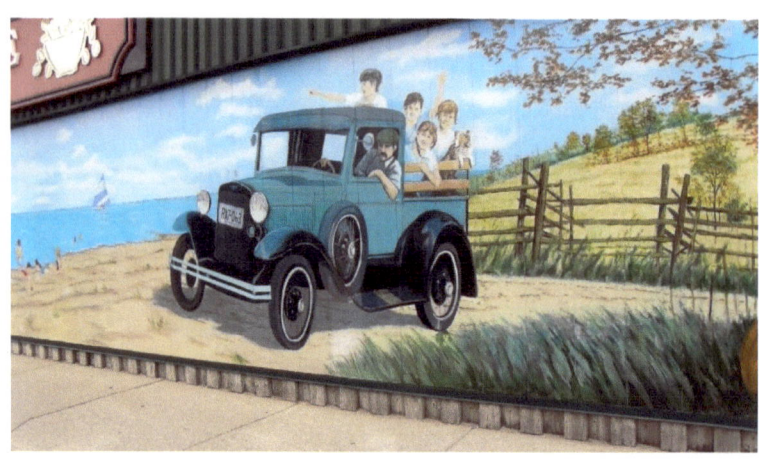

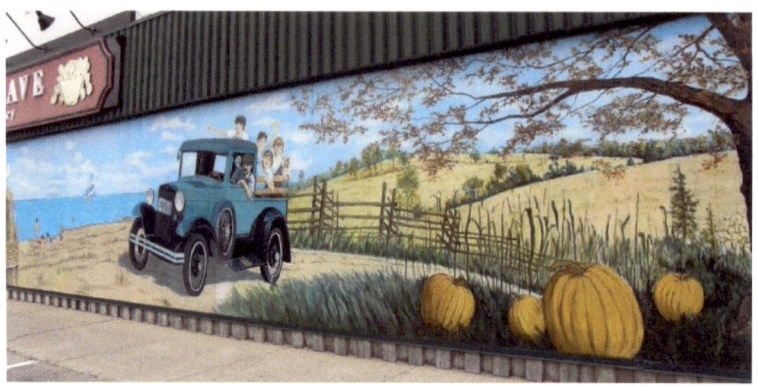

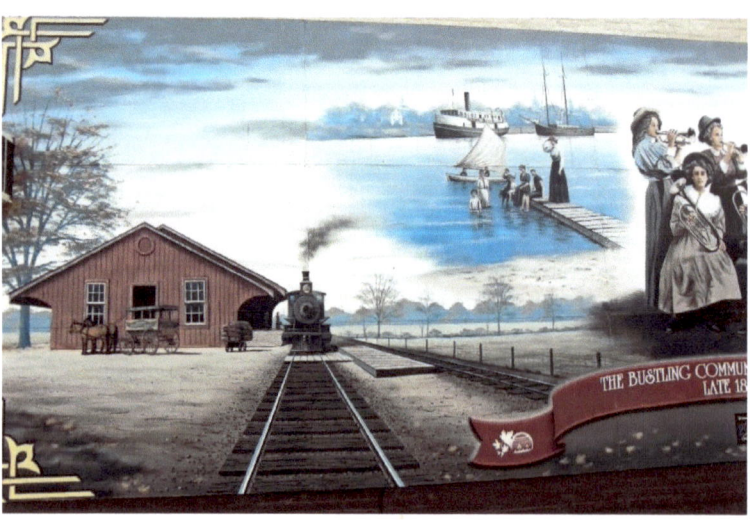

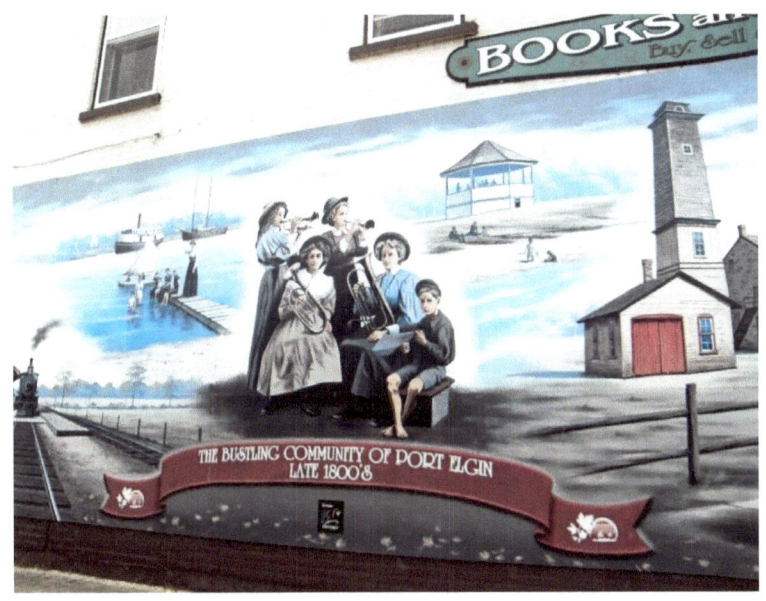

Murals

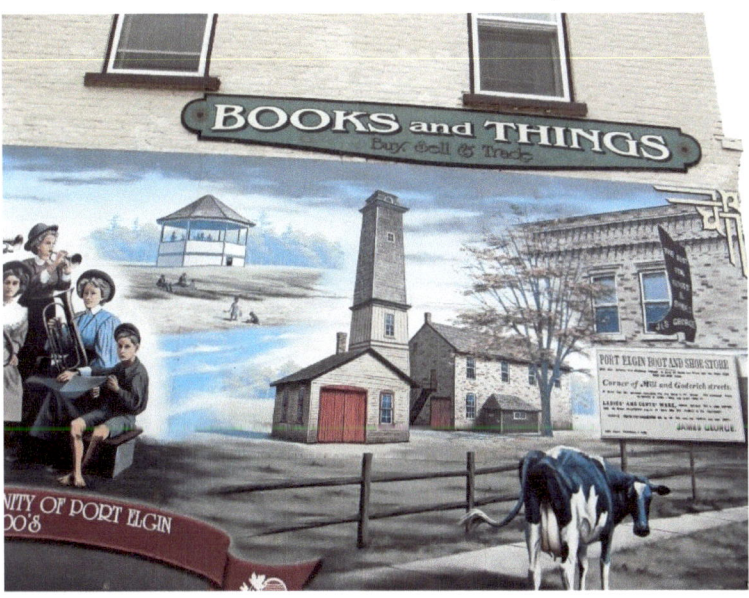

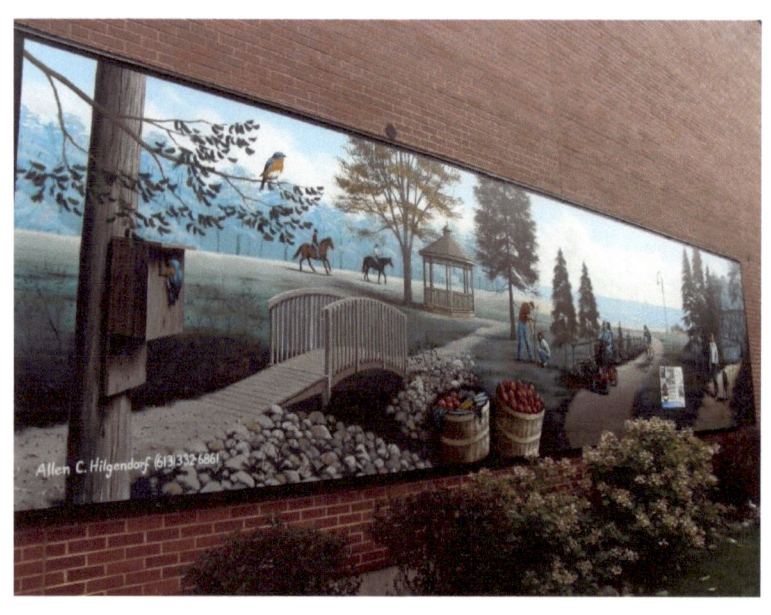

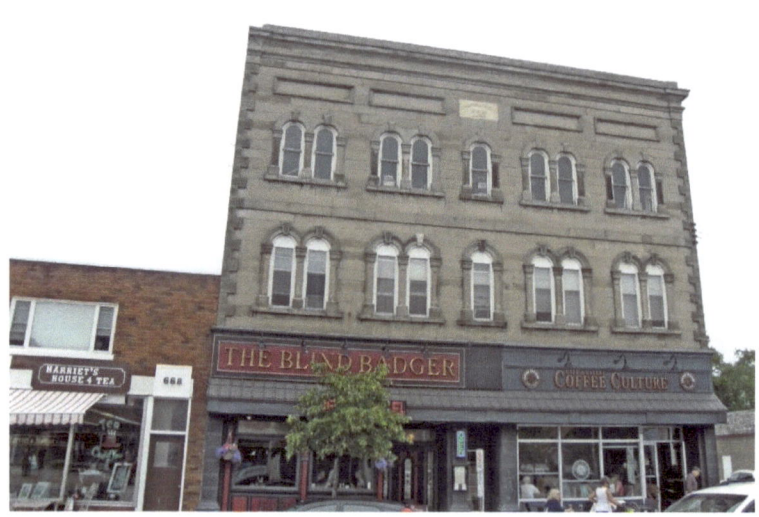

Decorative voussoirs and keystones
Commercial buildings erected A.D. 1878

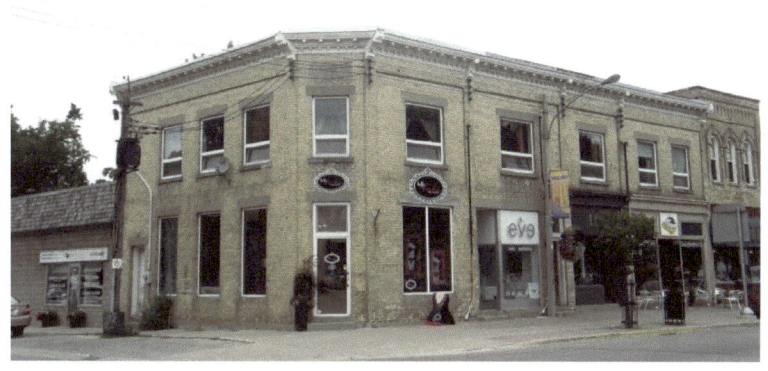

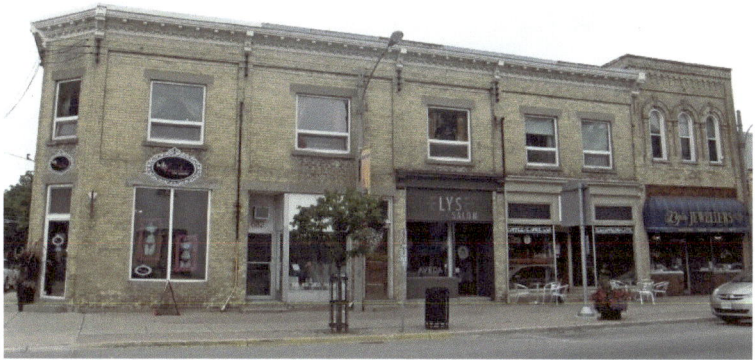

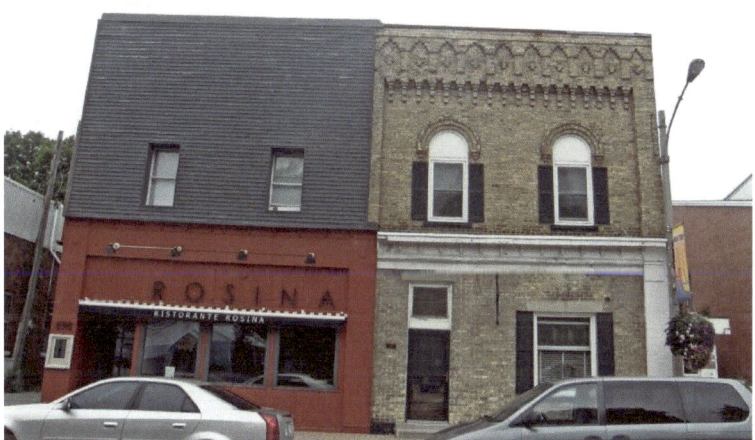

Decorative brickwork, arched window hoods

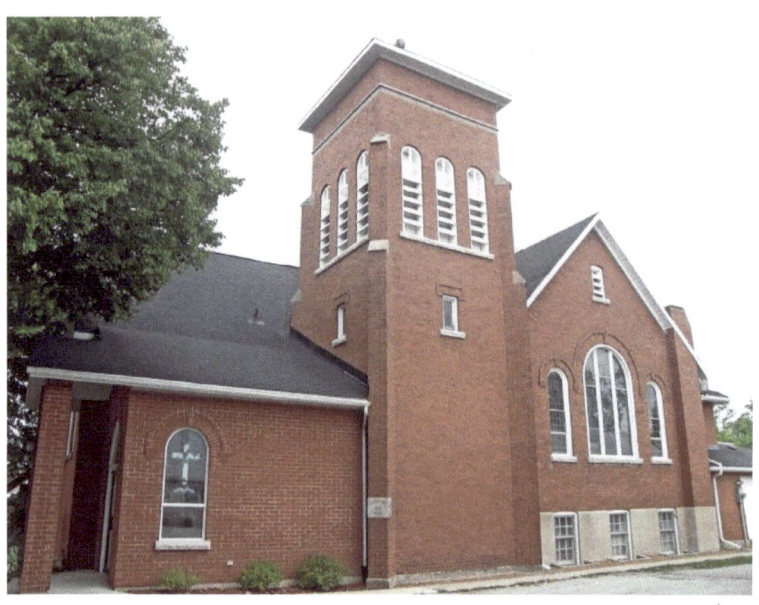

699 Goderich Street - Tolmie Memorial Presbyterian Church erected A.D. 1926 - red brick – Gothic Revival style – lancet windows, Romanesque style window arches

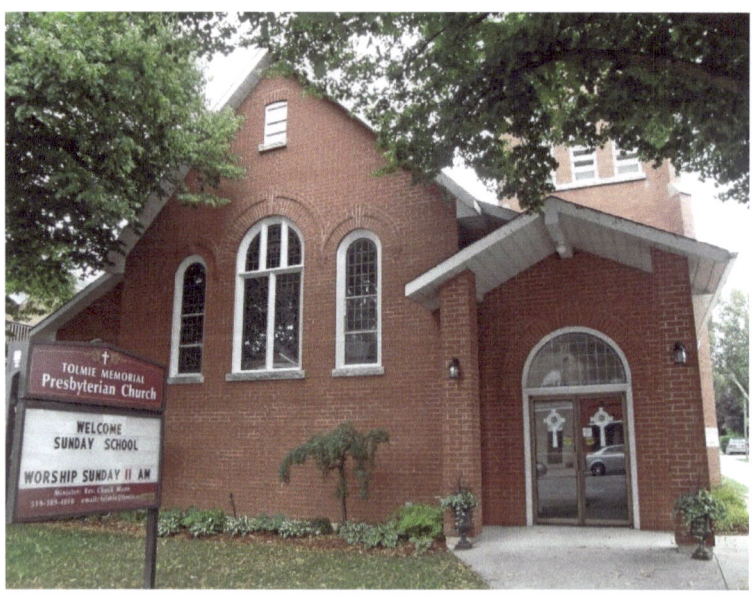

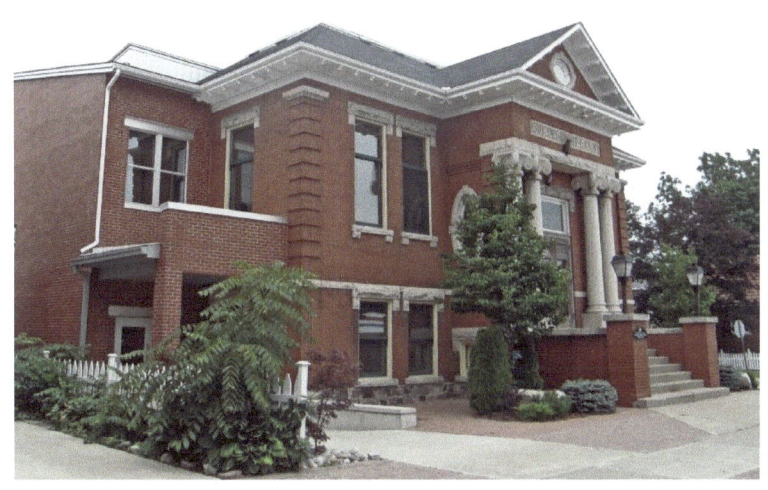

708 Goderich Street - Port Elgin Public Library

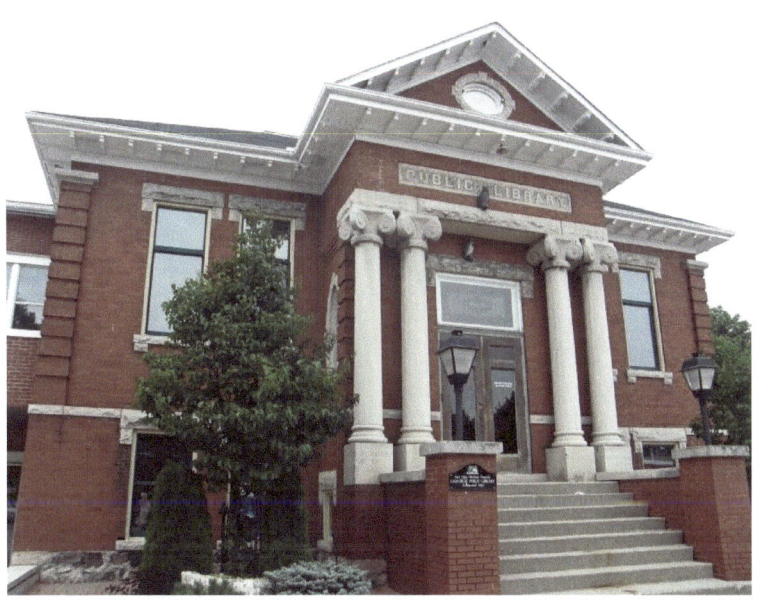

Beaux Arts style with frontispiece, round pillars with Ionic
capitals, triangular pediment with round window,
stone window lintels, corner quoins

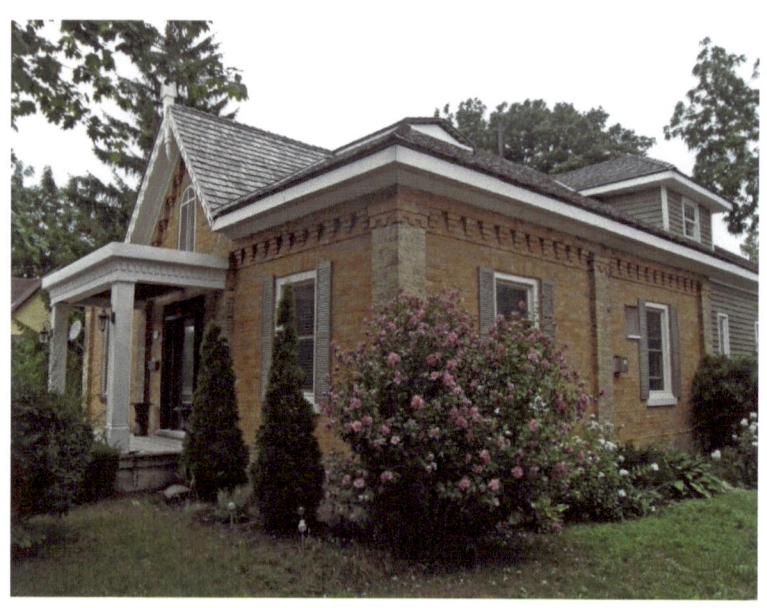

591 Elgin Street – Gothic Revival style, decorative brickwork in tympanum, bevelled dentil moulding below cornice, finial and trim on gable above front door, dormer in attic

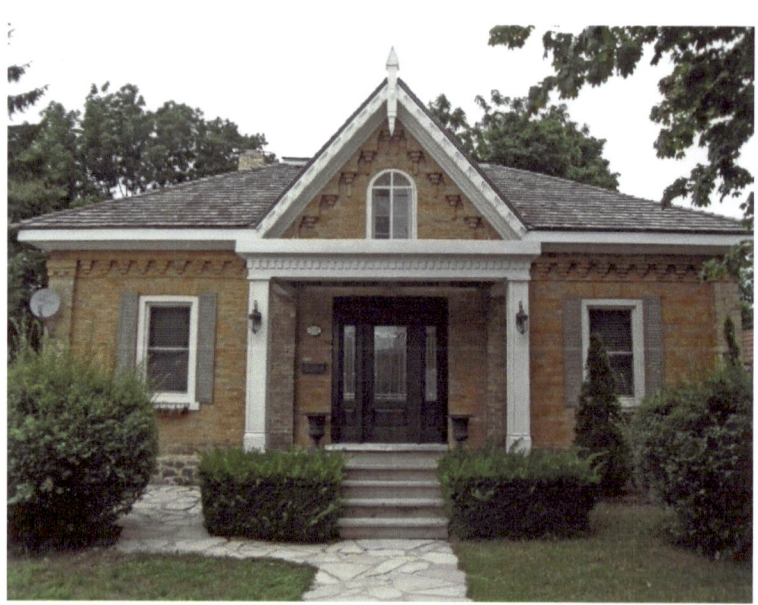

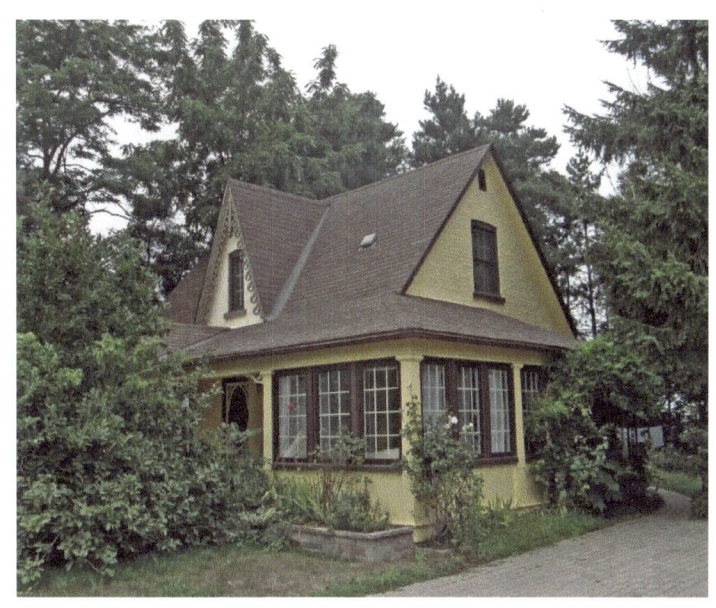

Gothic Cottage – Verge board trim on gable

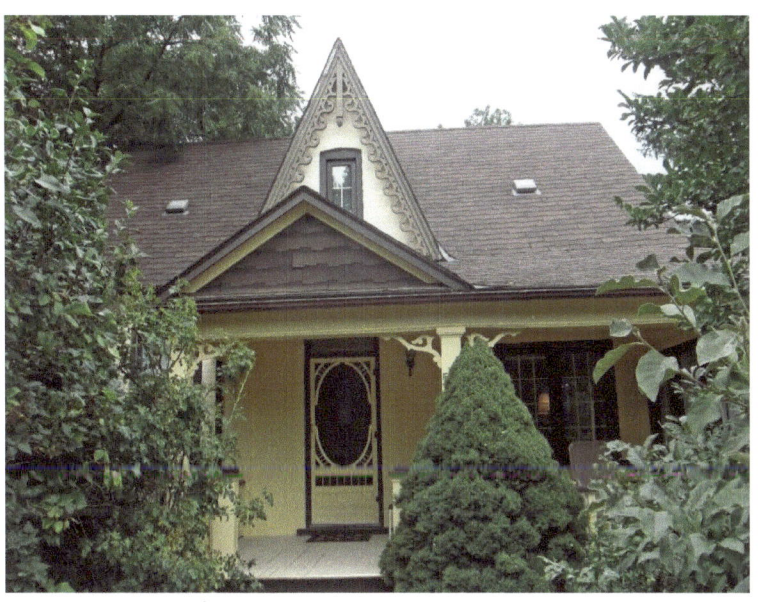

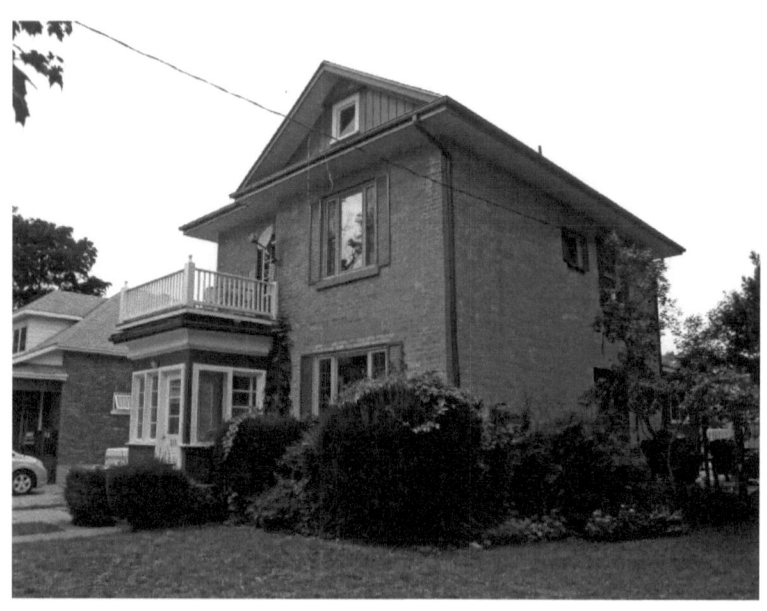

575 Elgin Street - Yellow brick, Italianate style, with gabled dormer in attic, 2nd floor balcony

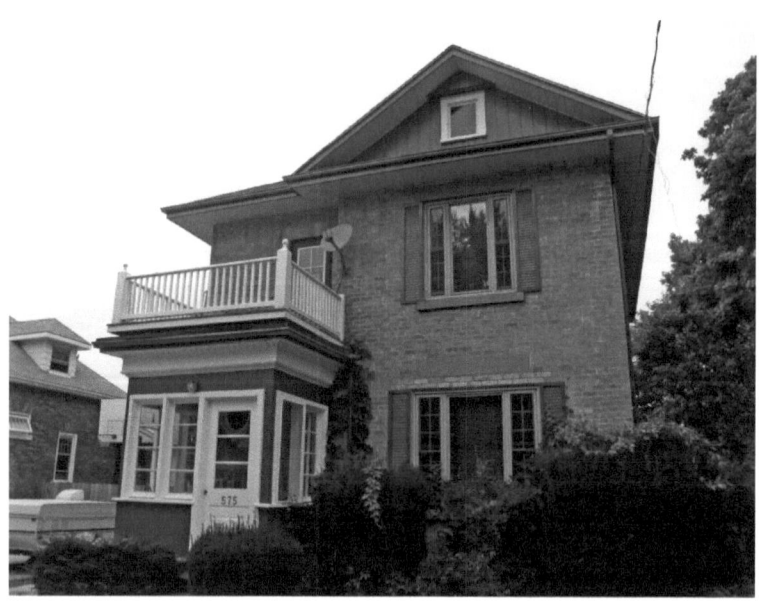

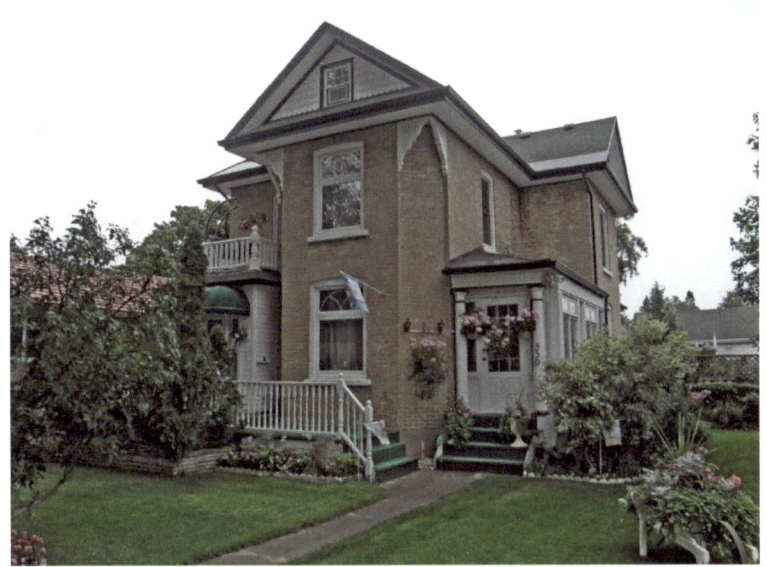

559 Elgin Street - fretwork resembling brackets under gable –
yellow brick which has lots of lime in it

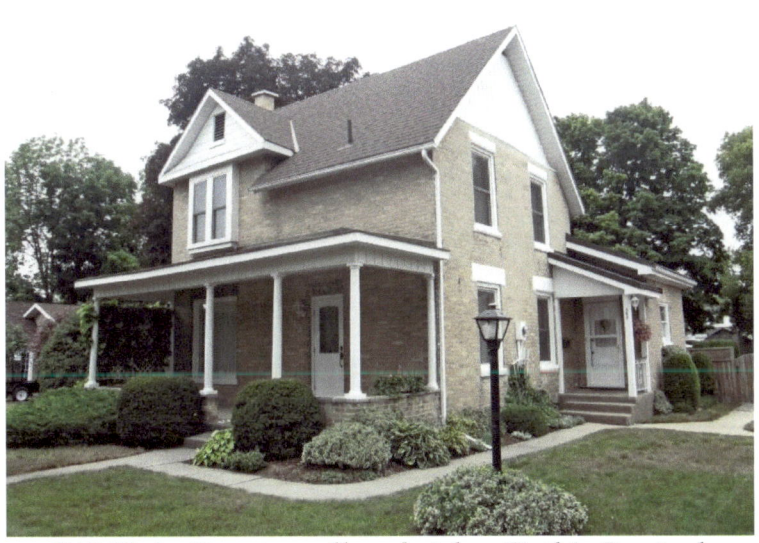

545 Elgin Street – yellow brick – Gothic Revival

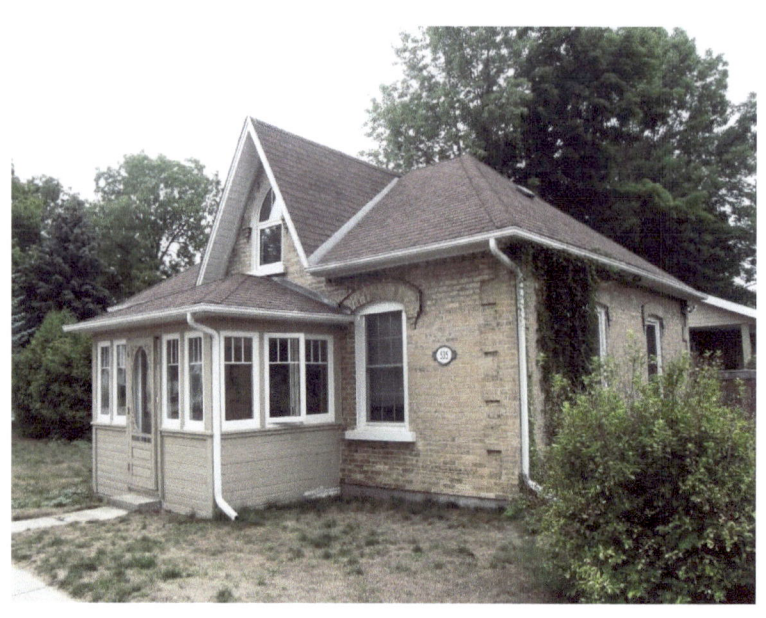

535 Elgin Street – yellow brick one storey Gothic cottage, decorative brick window voussoirs, corner quoins

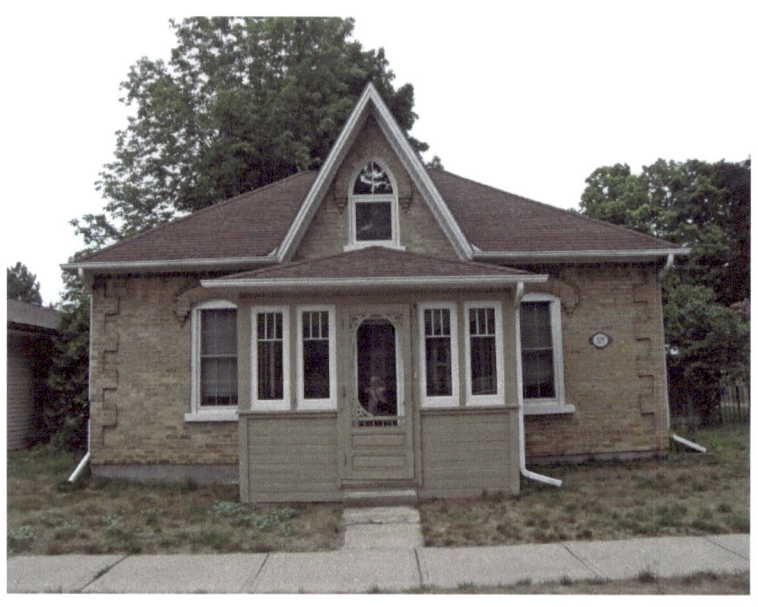

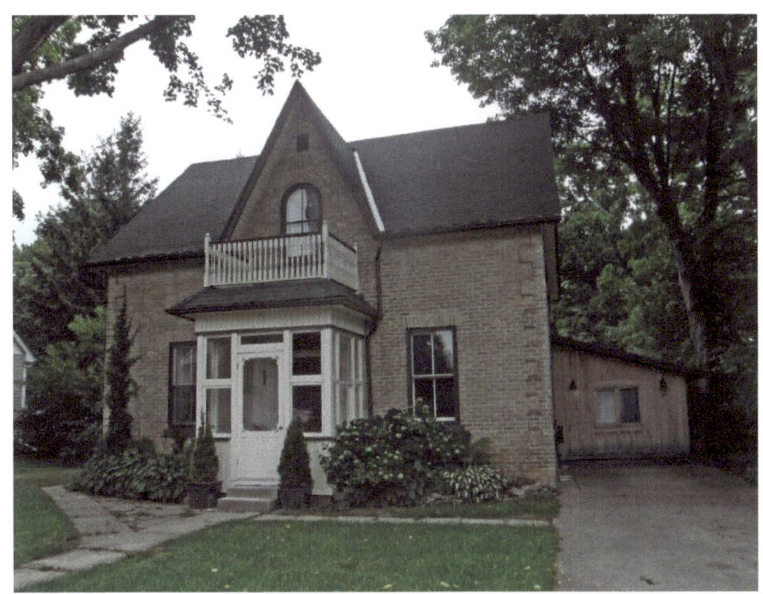

1½ storey Gothic Cottage with 2nd floor balcony

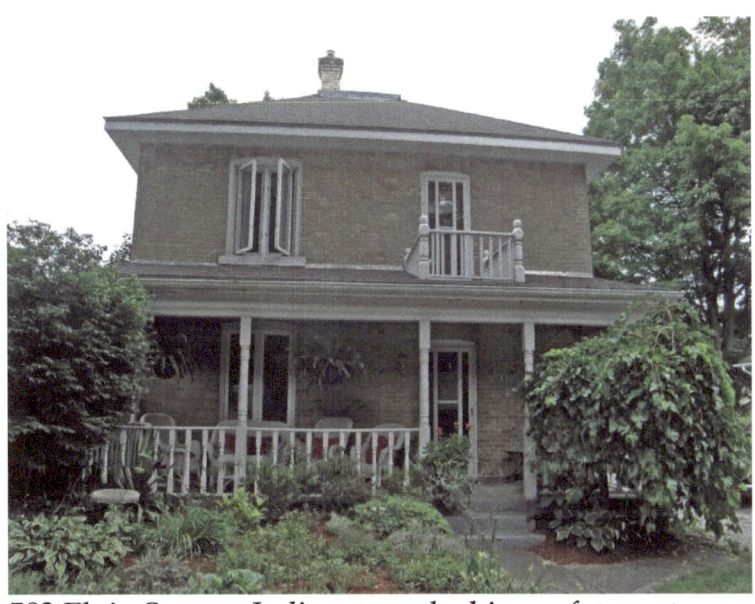

503 Elgin Street – Italianate style, hip roof, two storeys

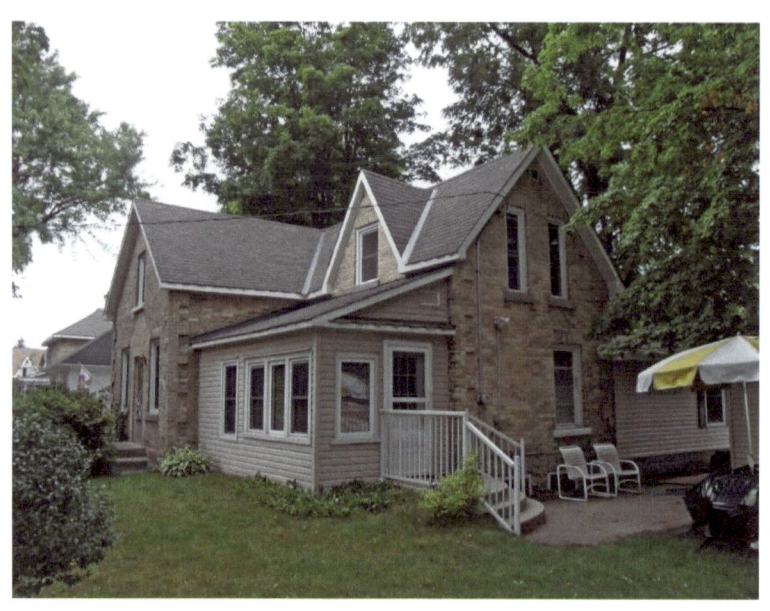

515 Elgin Street – Gothic, yellow brick, quoins

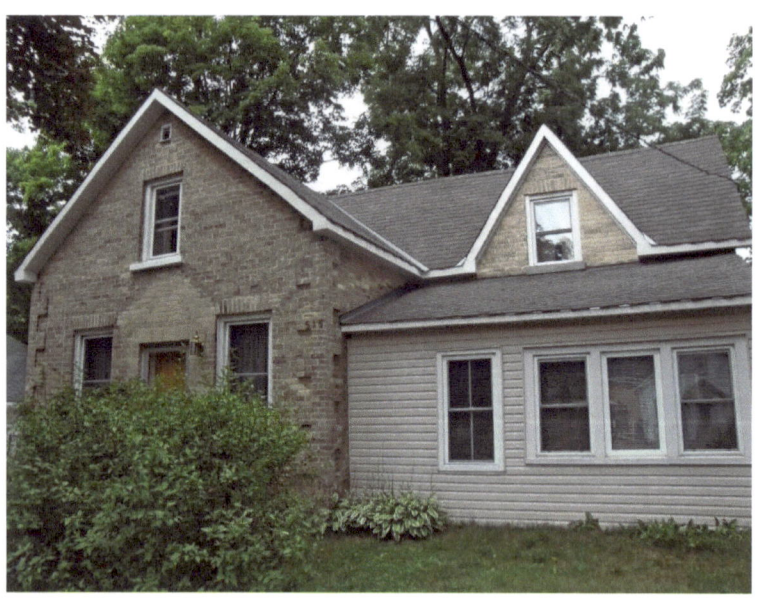

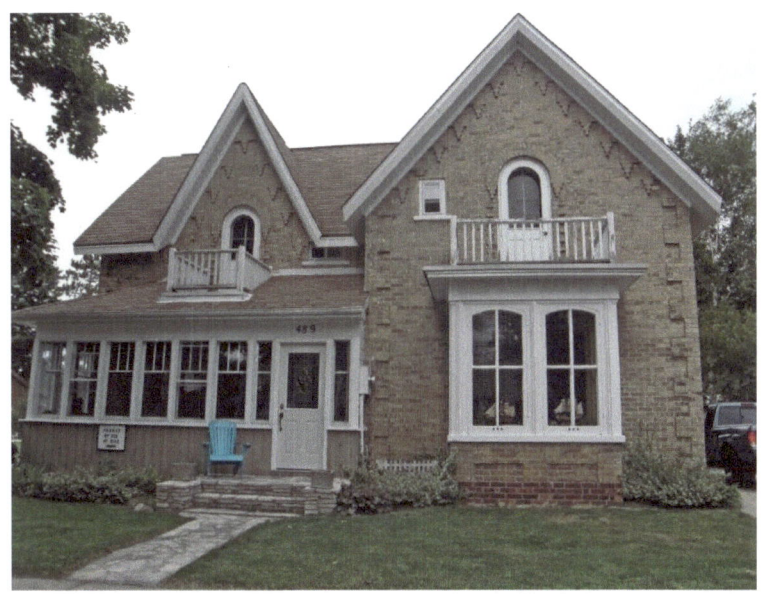

489 Elgin Street – Gothic Revival – bevelled dentil moulding under cornice, corner quoins, 2nd floor balconies

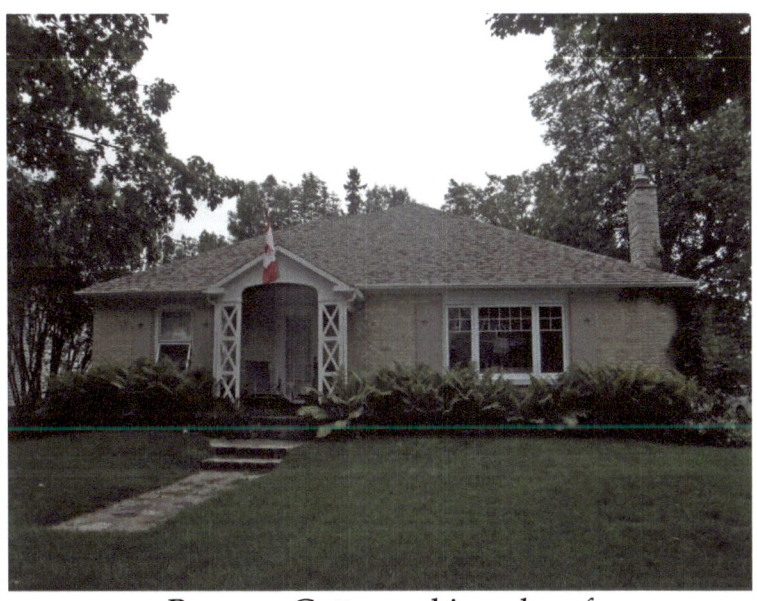

Regency Cottage – hipped roof

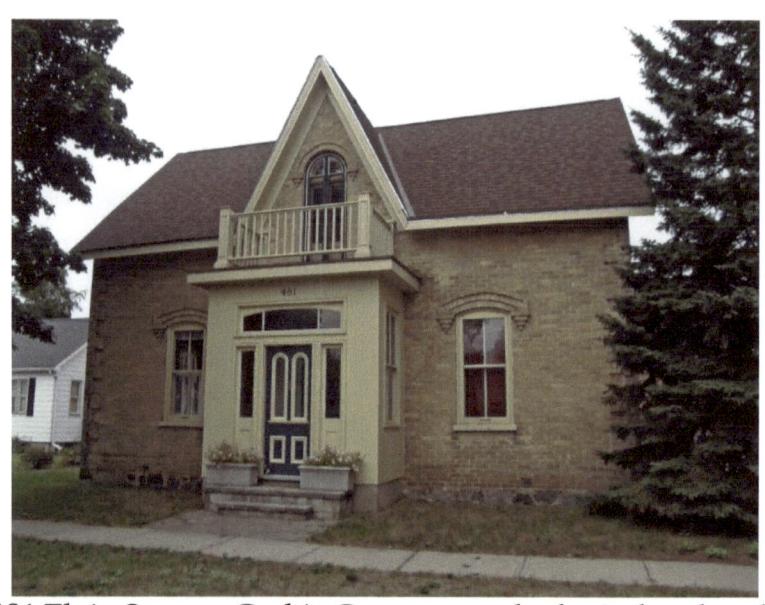

481 Elgin Street – Gothic Cottage – arched window hoods

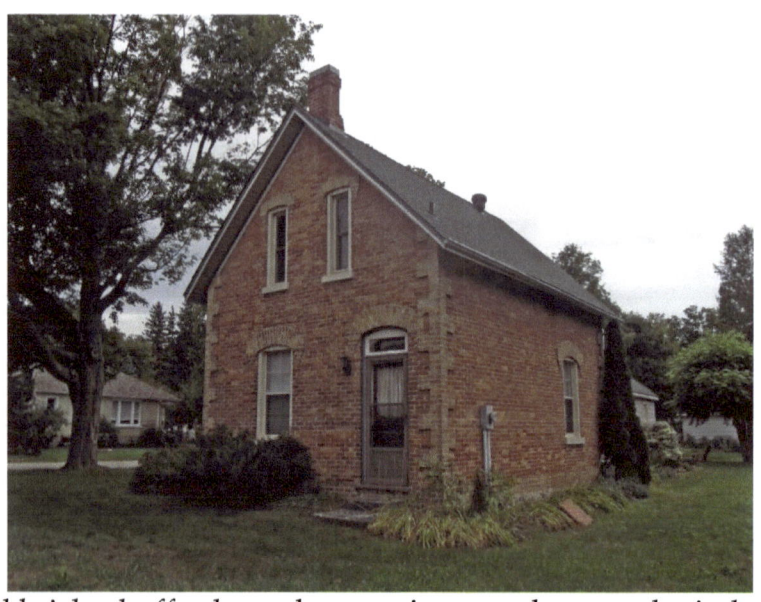

Red brick – buff coloured voussoirs over doors and windows, quoins on corners – Gothic Revival style

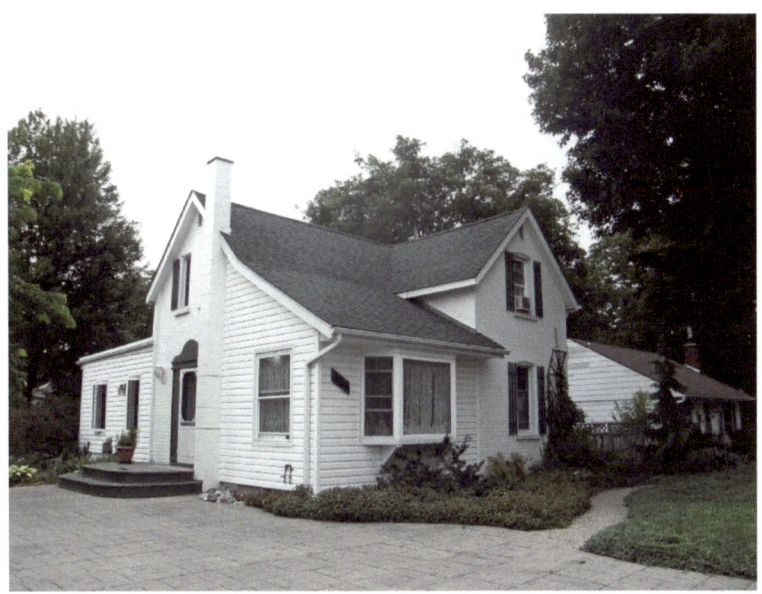

466 Elgin Street – Gothic Revival

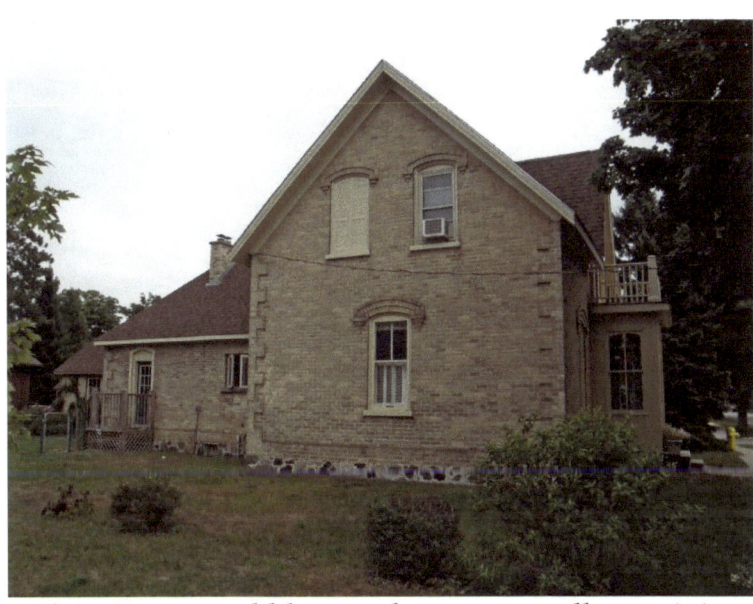

481 Elgin Street – cobblestone basement walls, quoining on corners, arched window voussoirs – yellow brick

Hepworth

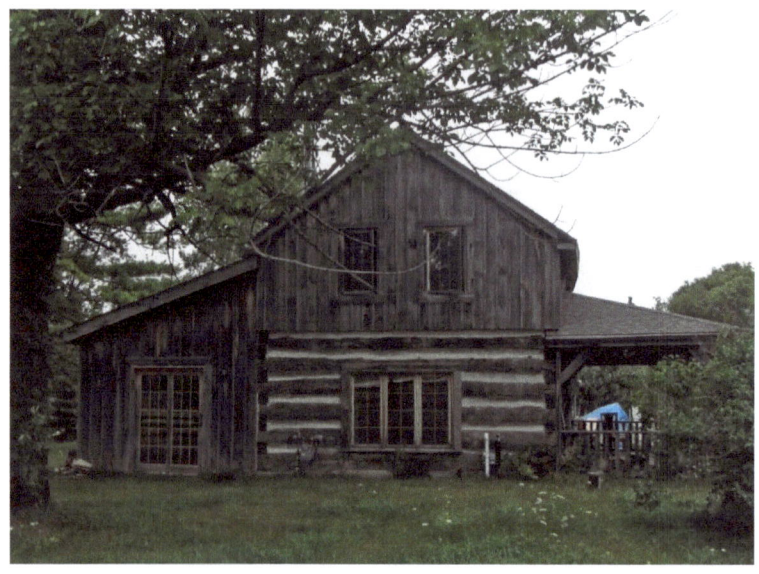

Log cabin

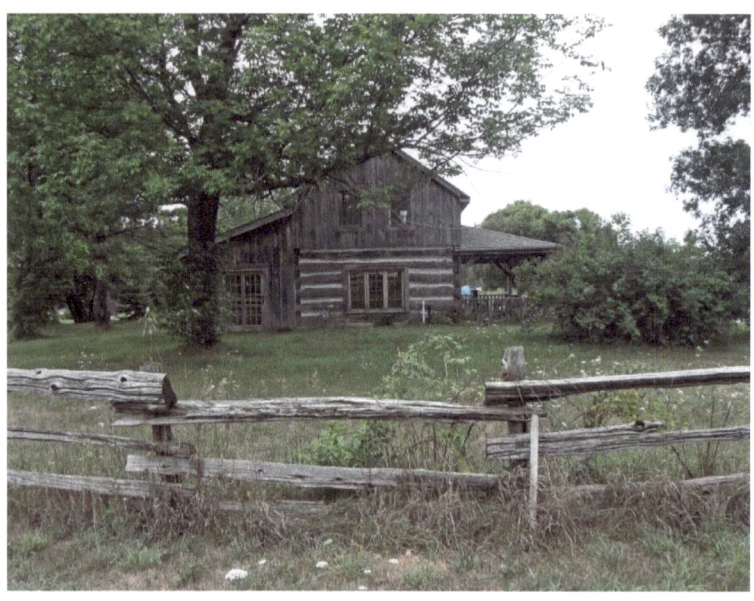

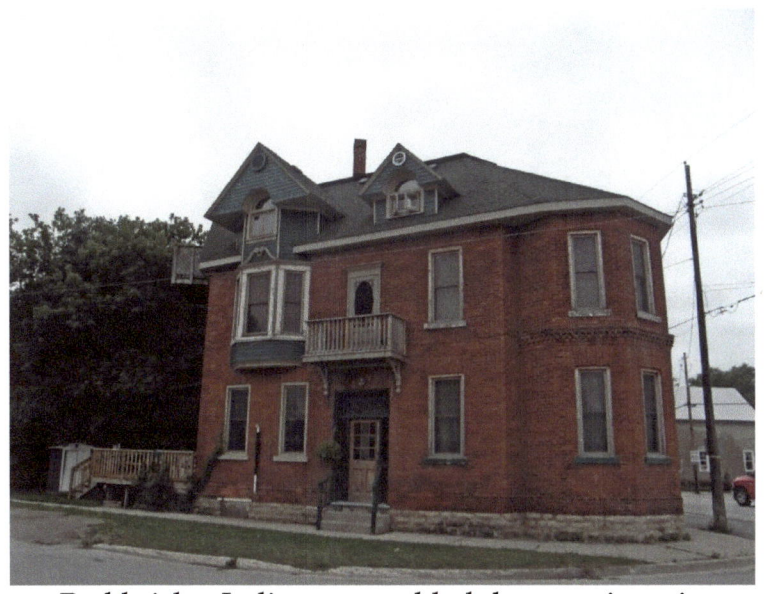

Red brick – Italianate – gabled dormers in attic,
2nd floor bay window, 2nd floor balcony

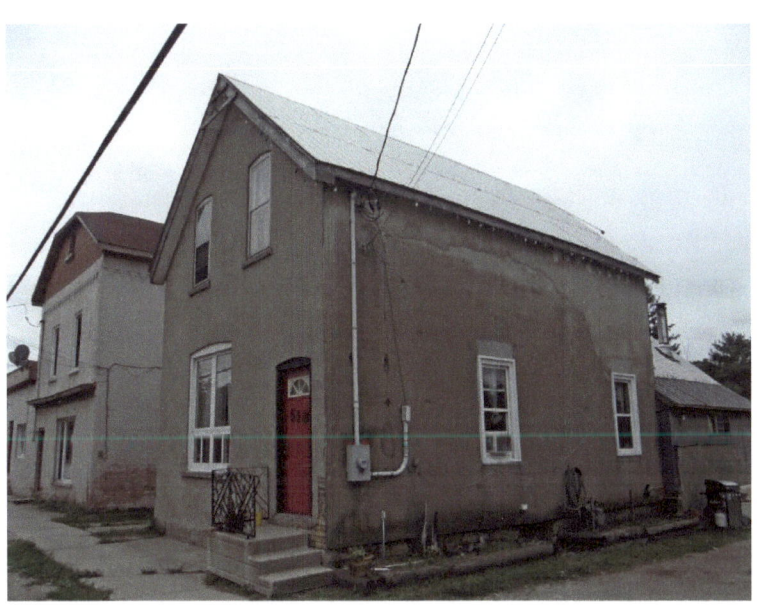

1½ storey Gothic cottage with plaster exterior

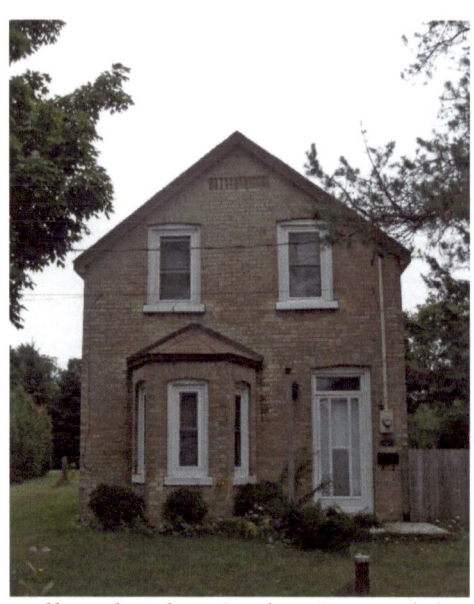

1½ storey yellow brick – Gothic Revival, bay window

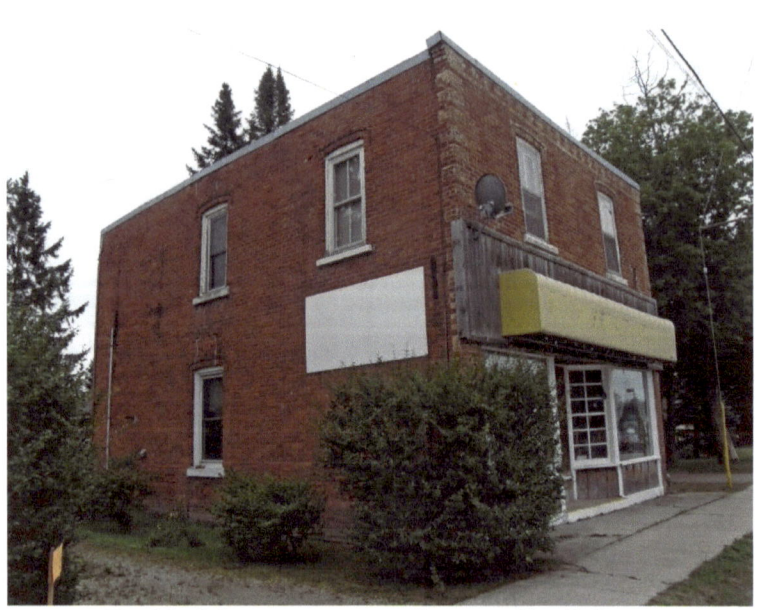

Red brick two-storey, flat roof building,
dichromatic brickwork

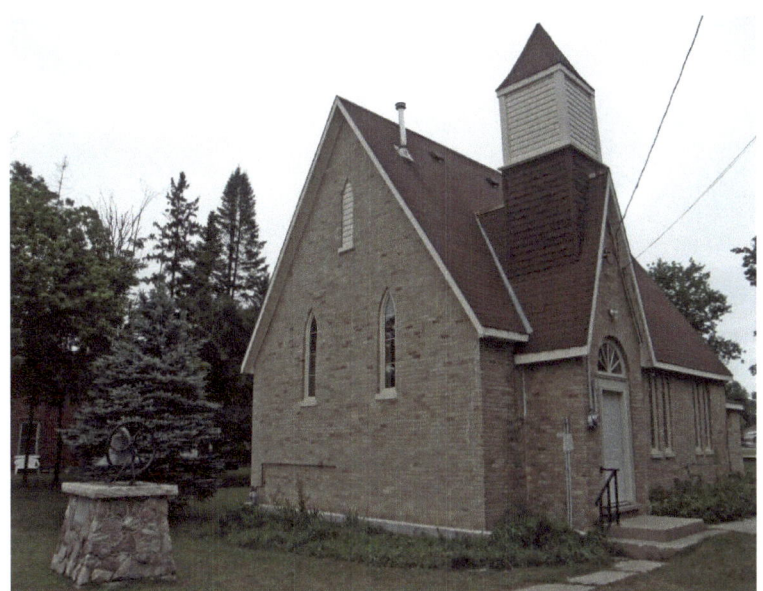

Anglican Church of the Redeemer – built 1886. From 1965 to 1997 it was the public library. In January 1998 it became the Community Centre for the village of Hepworth.

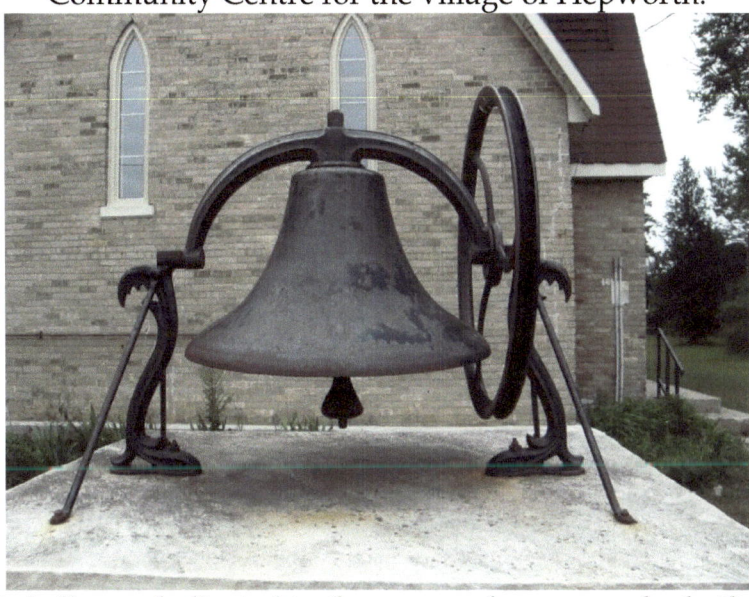

This bell was dedicated to the men and women who built the Anglican Church of the Redeemer from 1886 through 1965.

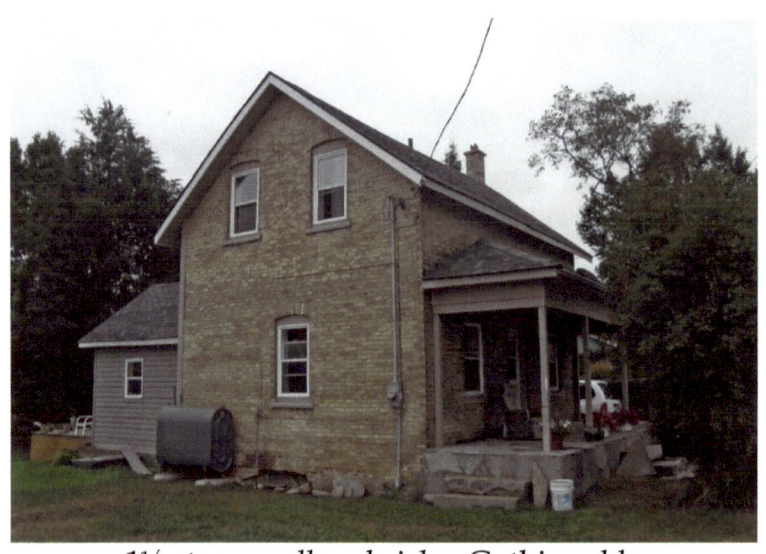

1½ storey yellow brick – Gothic gable

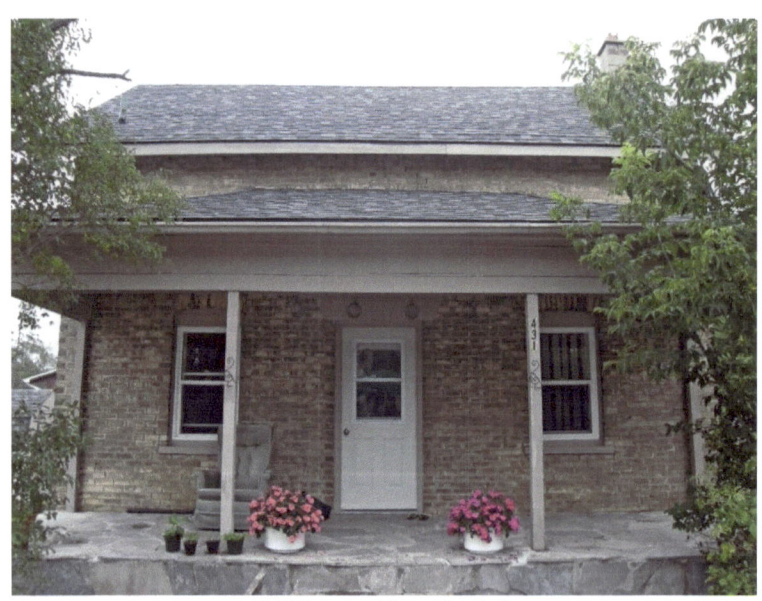

#431 – yellow brick

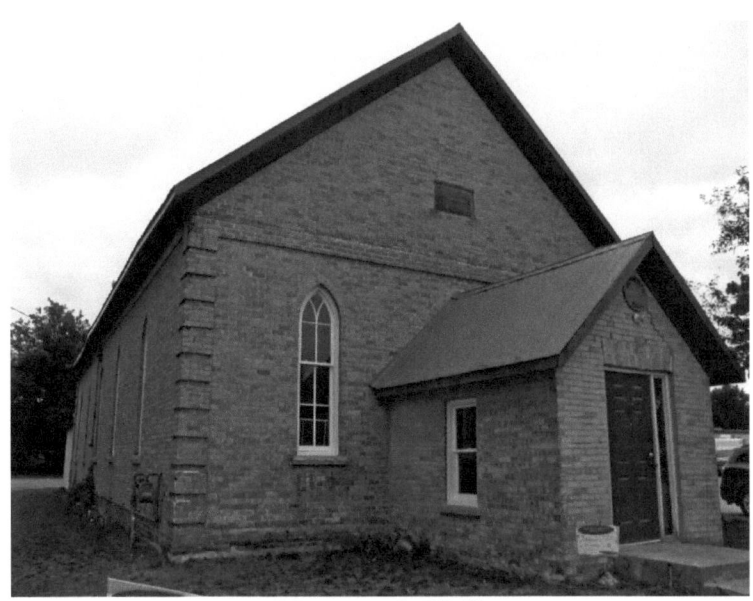

Hepworth Hall

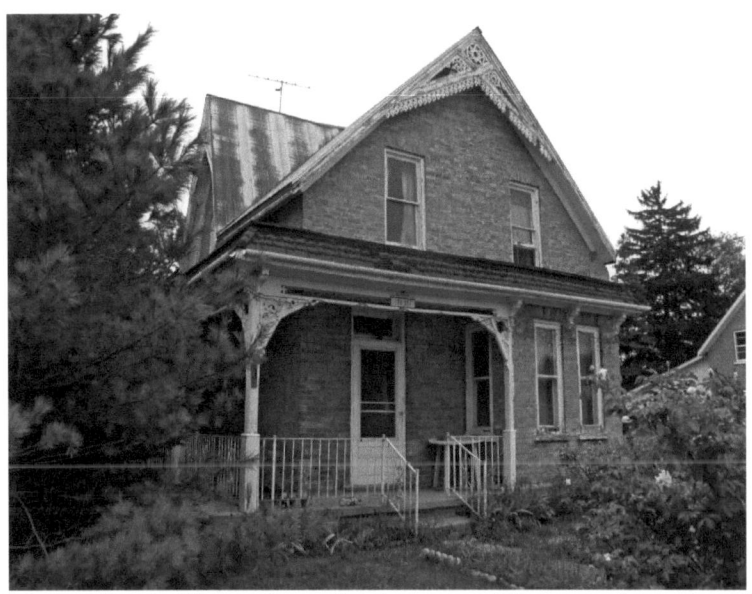

Gothic Revival –Verge board trim on gable, metal roof, yellow
brick, decorative brackets on verandah cornice

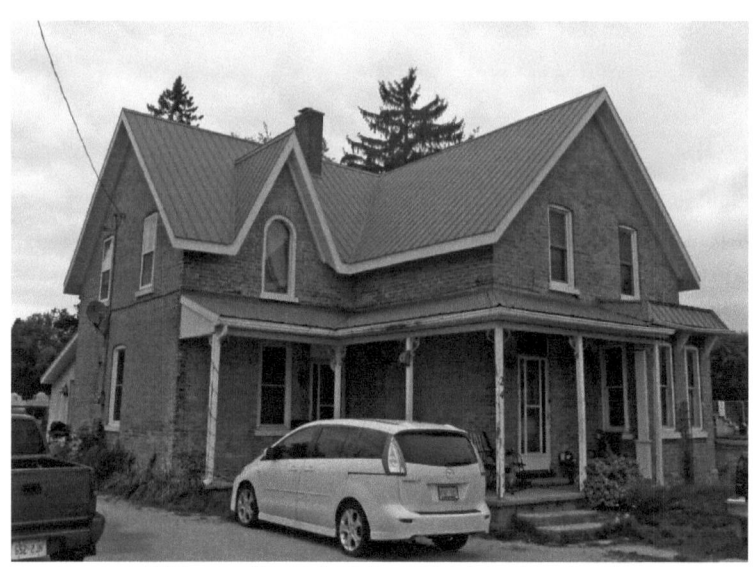

#24 – yellow brick – Gothic Revival

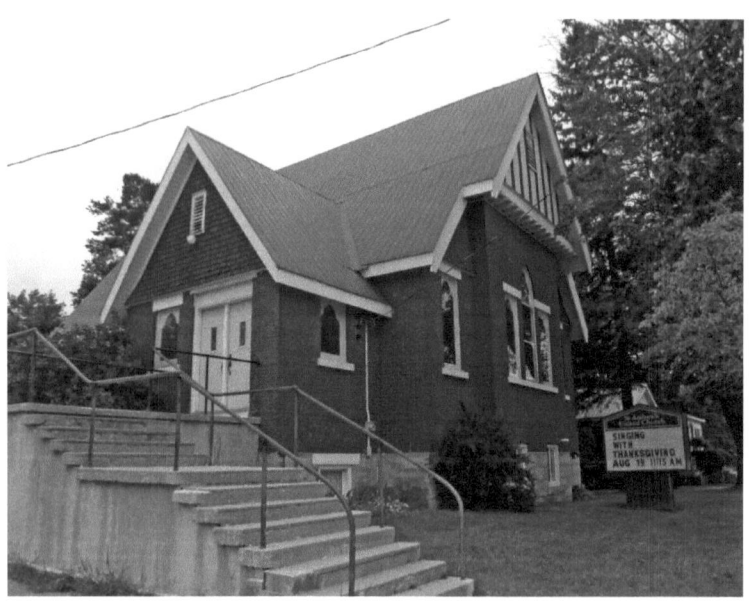

St. Andrew's United Church – red brick

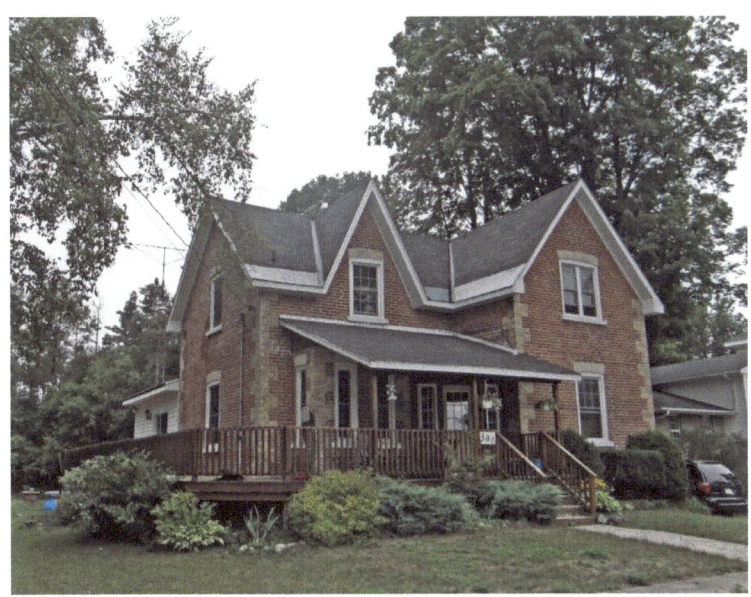

#480 – Gothic Revival – dichromatic brickwork, buff-coloured
window hoods

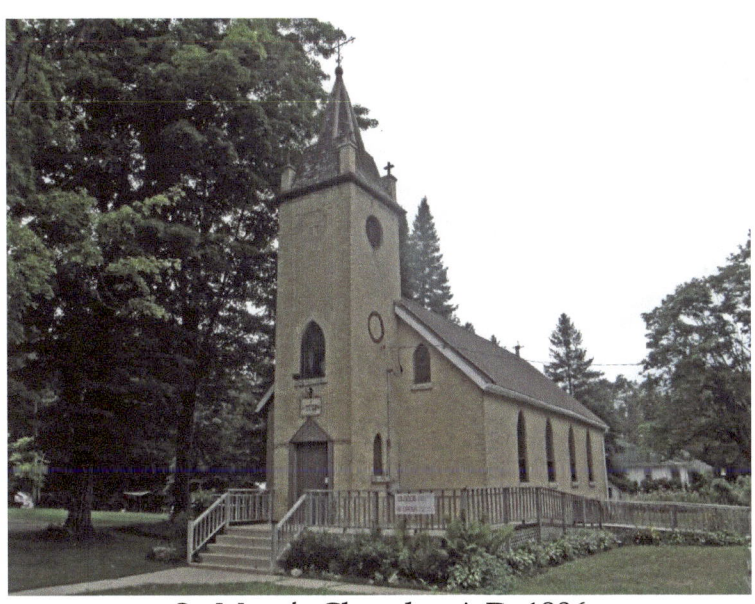

St. Mary's Church – A.D. 1906

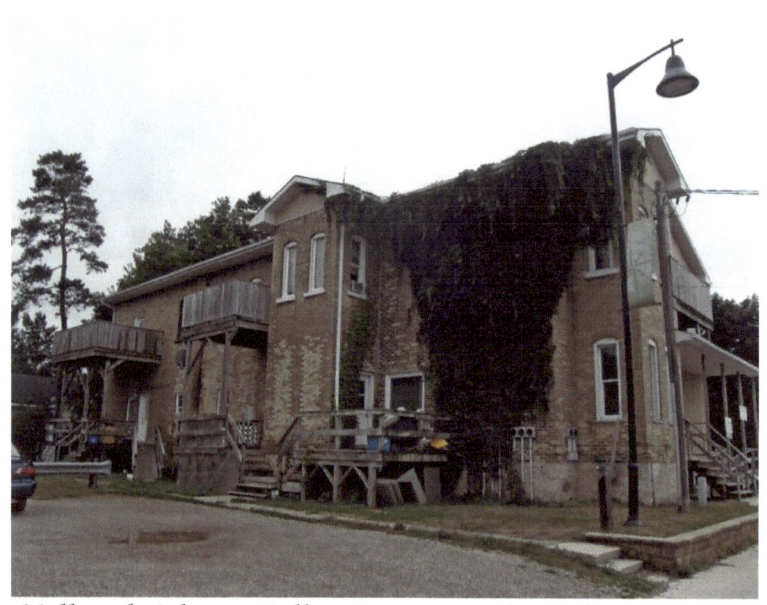

Yellow brick, partially vine covered – Italianate style

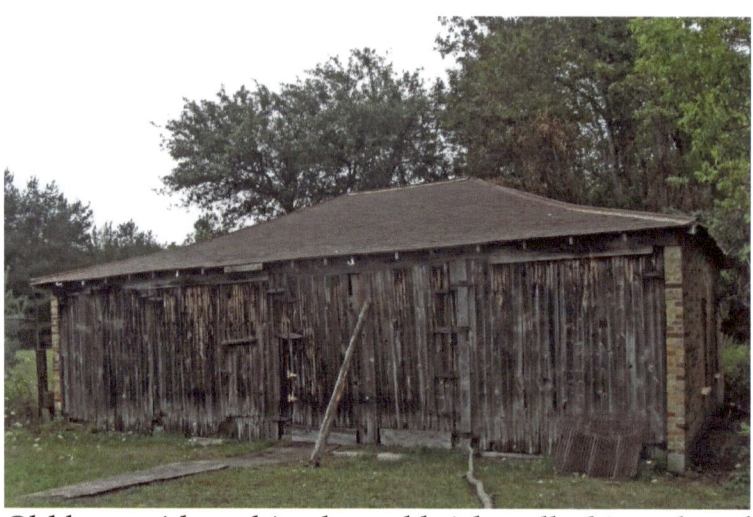

Old barn with multi-coloured brick walls, hipped roof

Sauble Beach

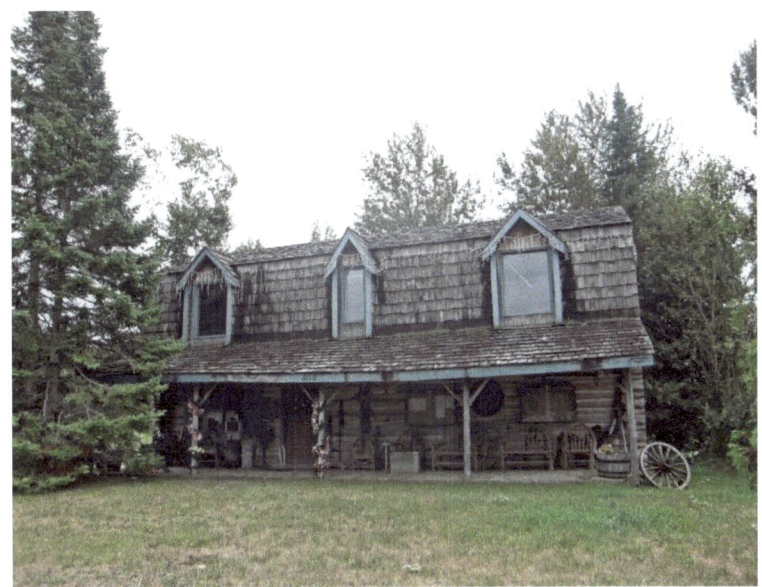

#808 – cedar shake roof, log cabin

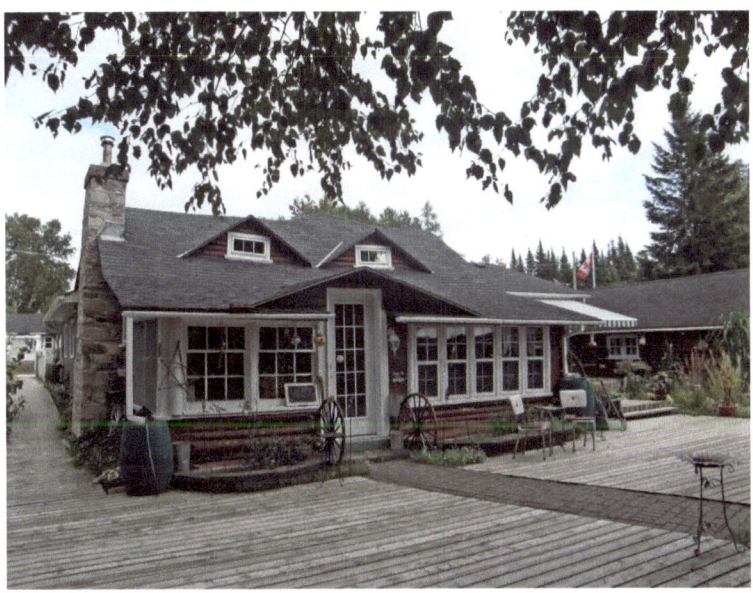

1930 log cabin – selling antiques

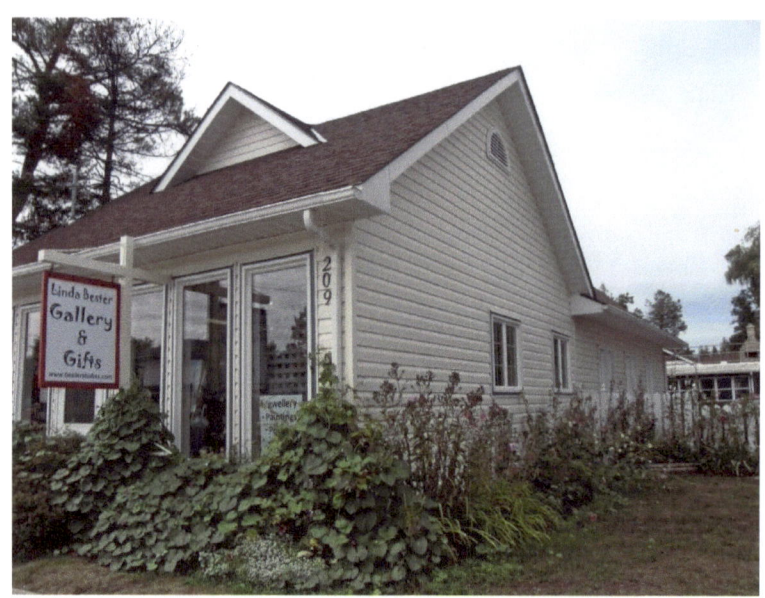

#209 – Gothic style with end gable

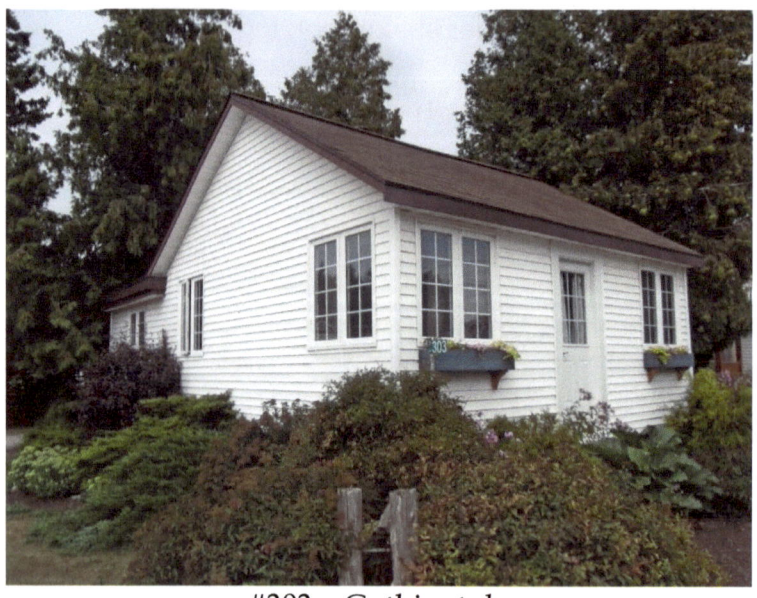

#303 – Gothic style

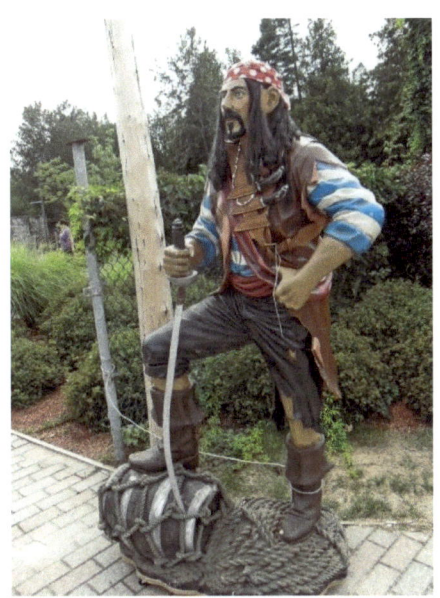

Pirate

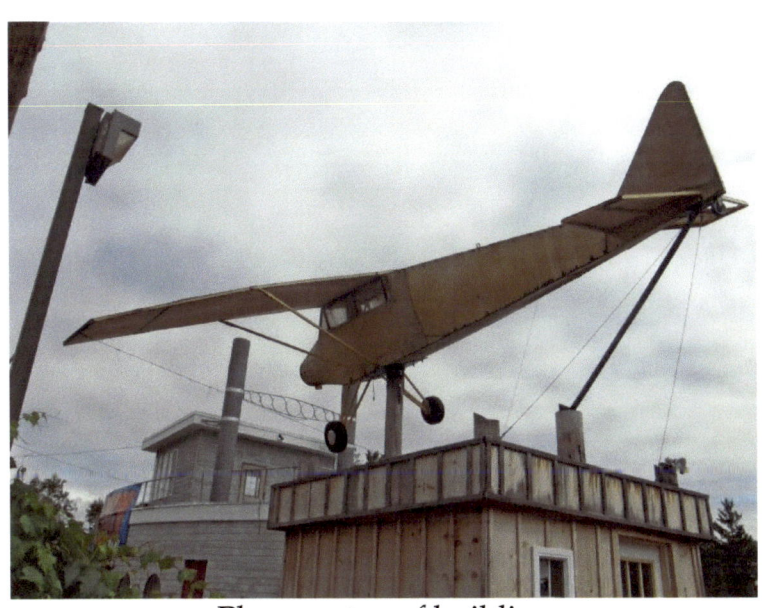

Plane on top of building

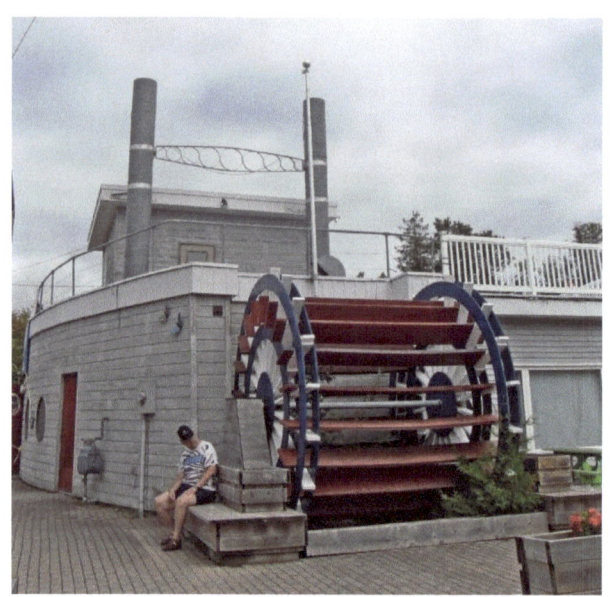

Paddle wheeler

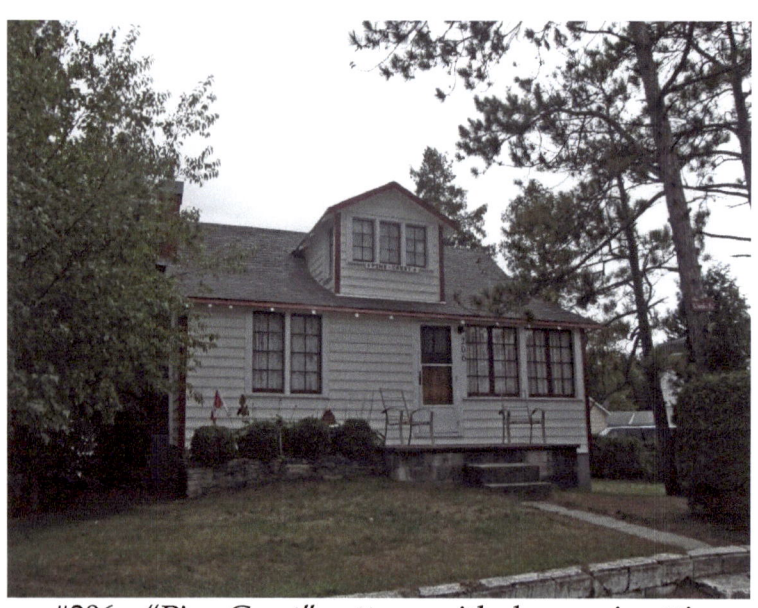

#206 – "Pine Crest" cottage with dormer in attic

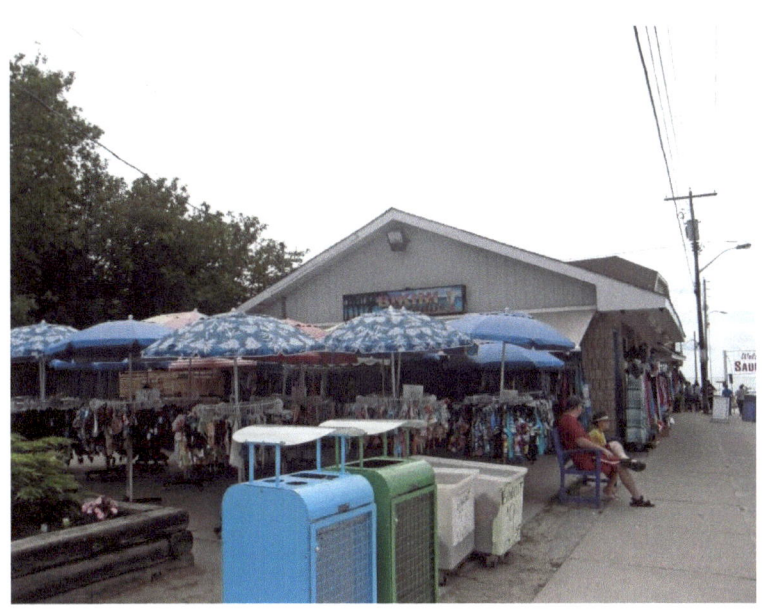

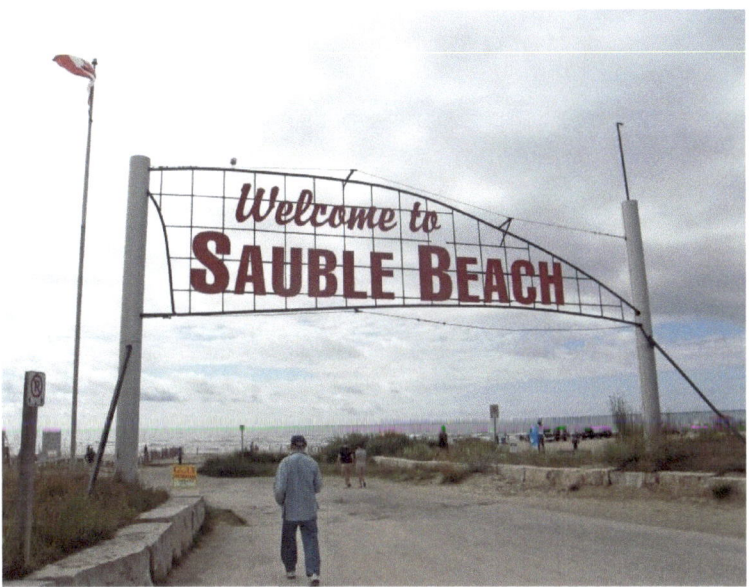

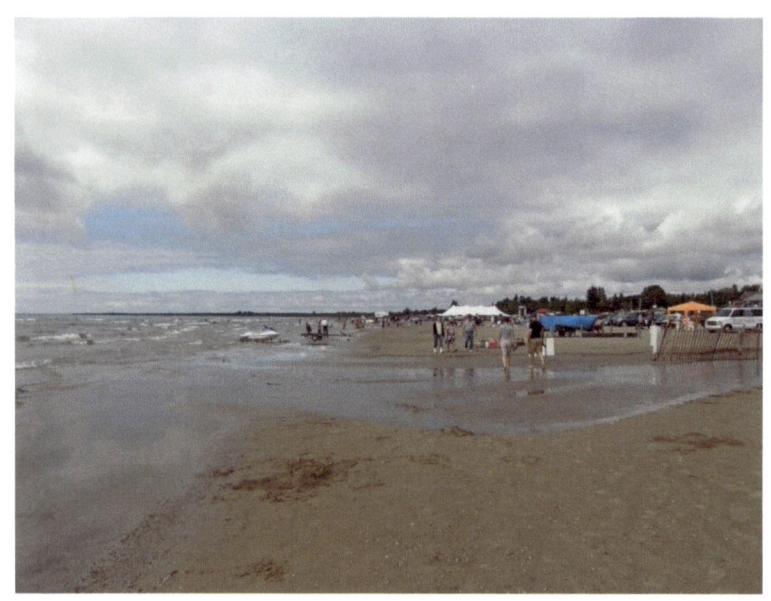

Shallow Lake

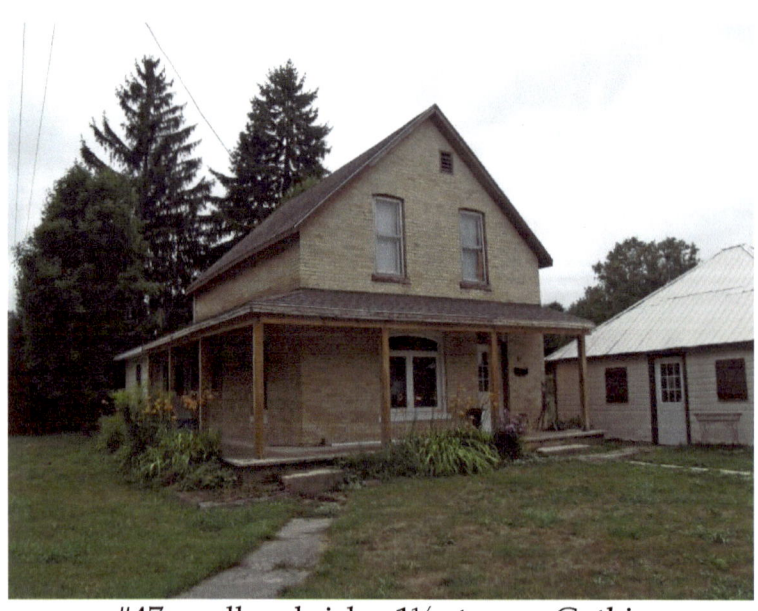

#47 – yellow brick – 1½ storey - Gothic

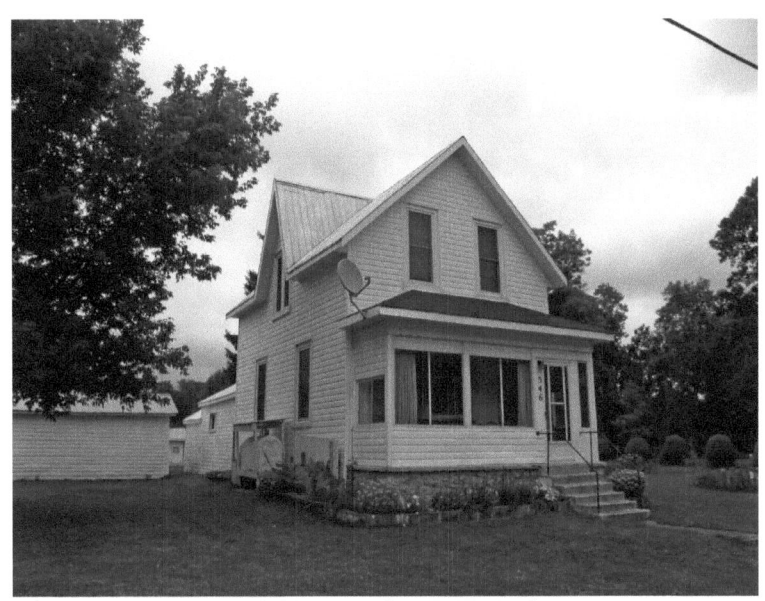

#346 – Gothic Revival

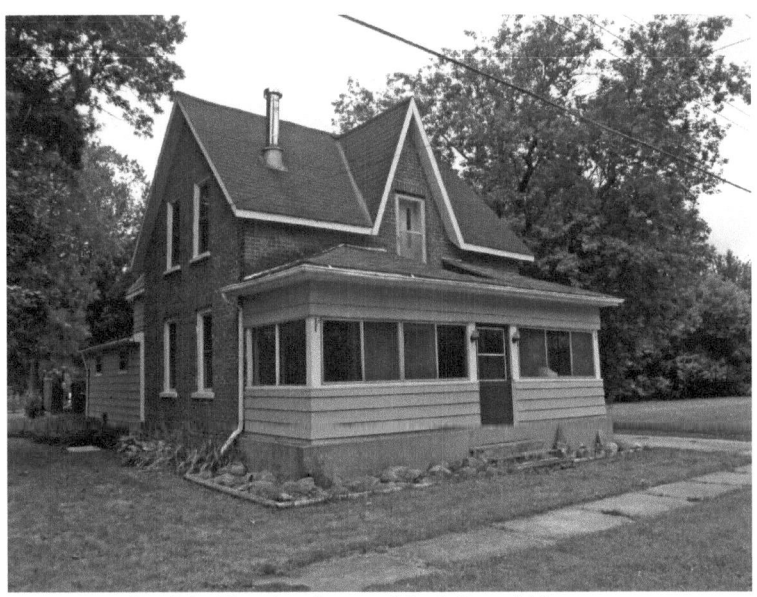

Gothic Revival – red brick – 1½ storey

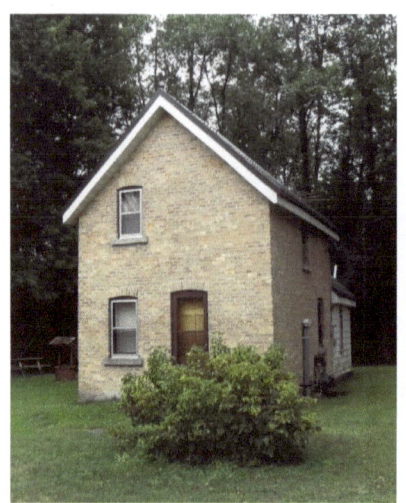 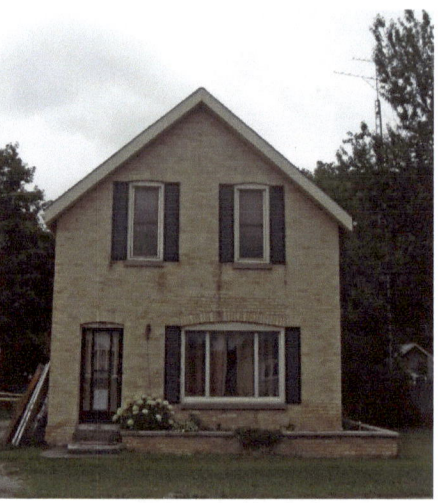

Gothic – yellow brick   #233 - Yellow brick

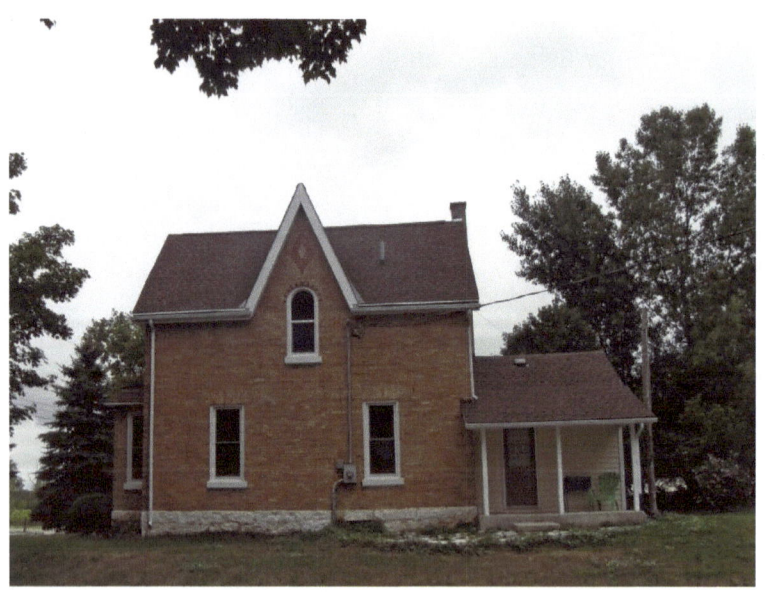

Gothic Revival - yellow-orange brick,
dichromatic brickwork decoration in the gable

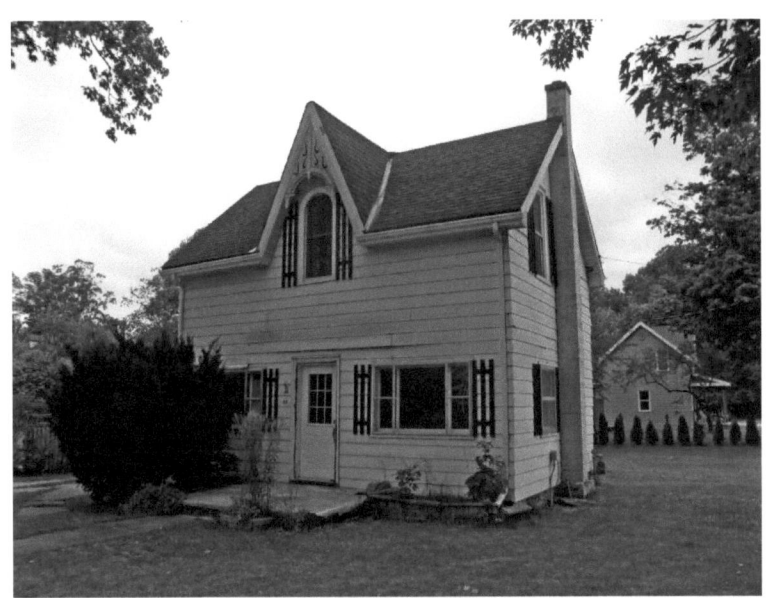

#35 – Gothic Revival – 1½ storey – Verge board trim on gable

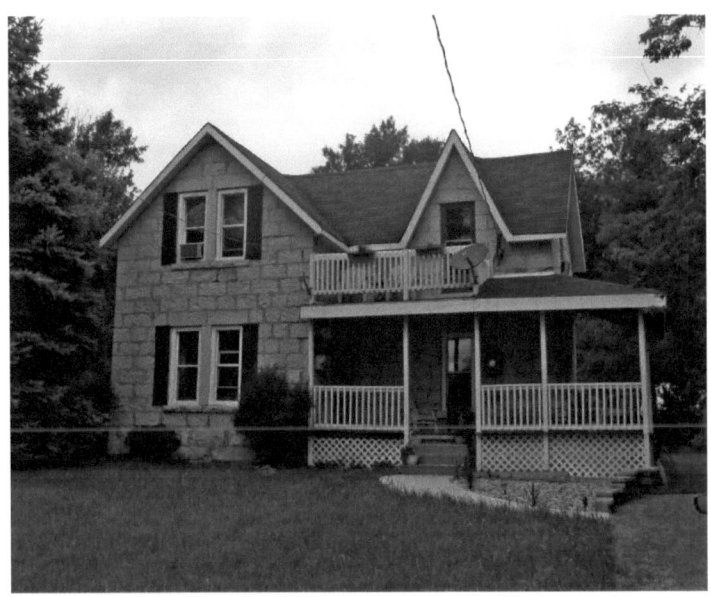

Gothic Revival – 1½ storey in limestone

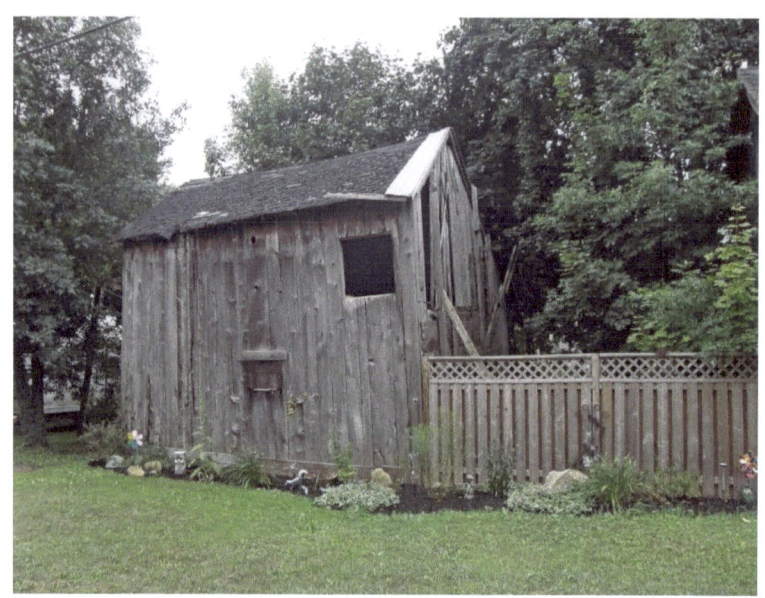

Old wooden barn

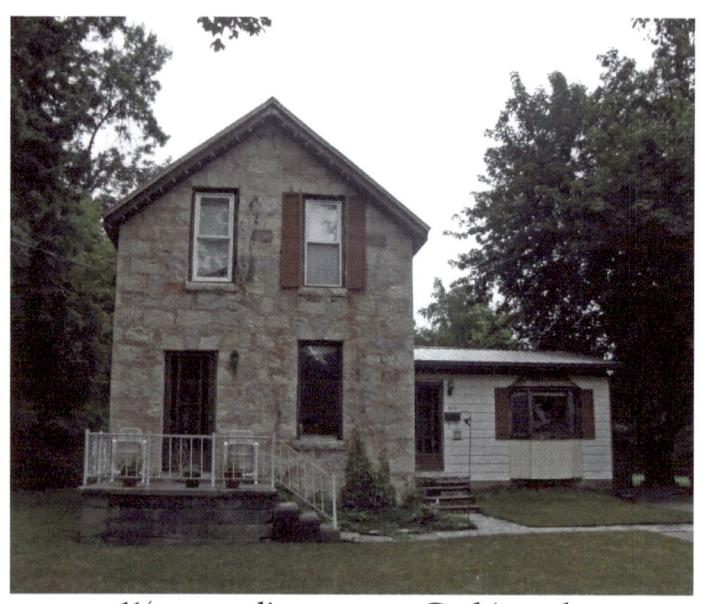

1½ storey limestone – Gothic style

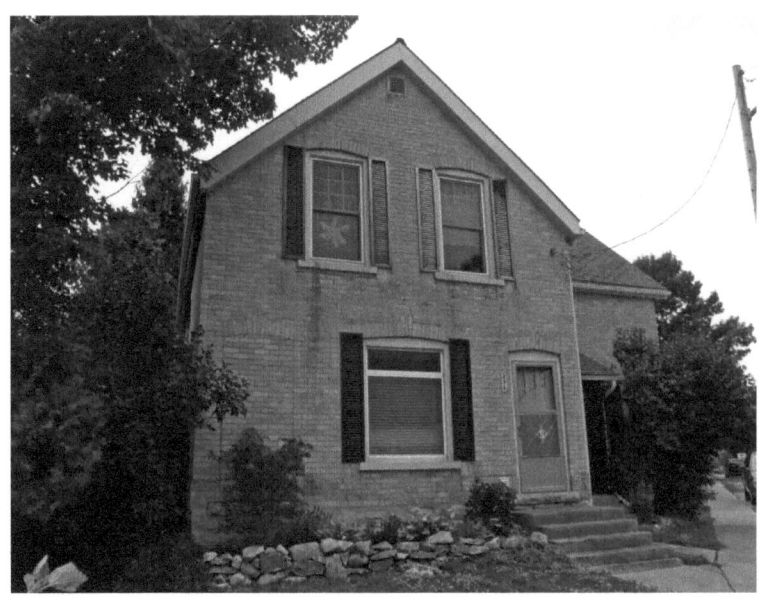

#256 – yellow brick - Gothic

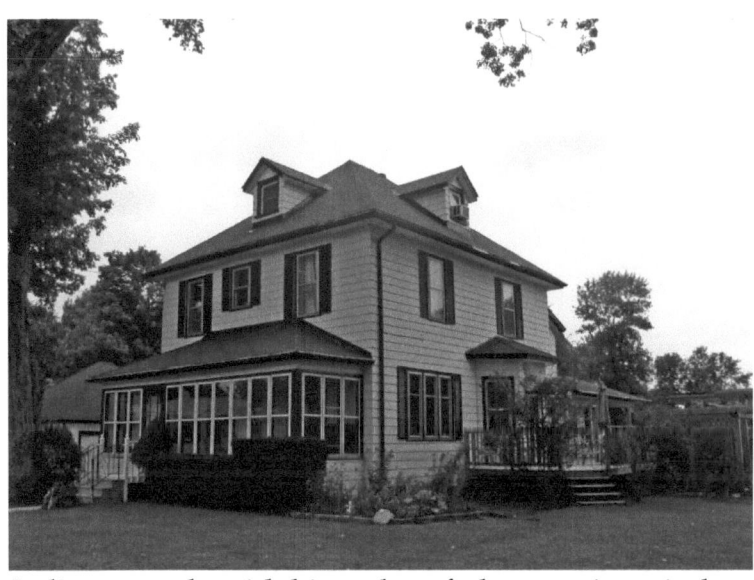

Italianate style with hipped roof, dormers in attic, bay window on side of house

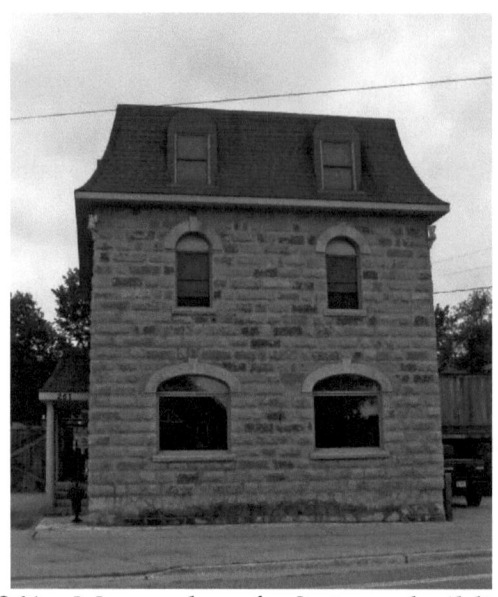

#261 – Mansard roof – 3 storey building

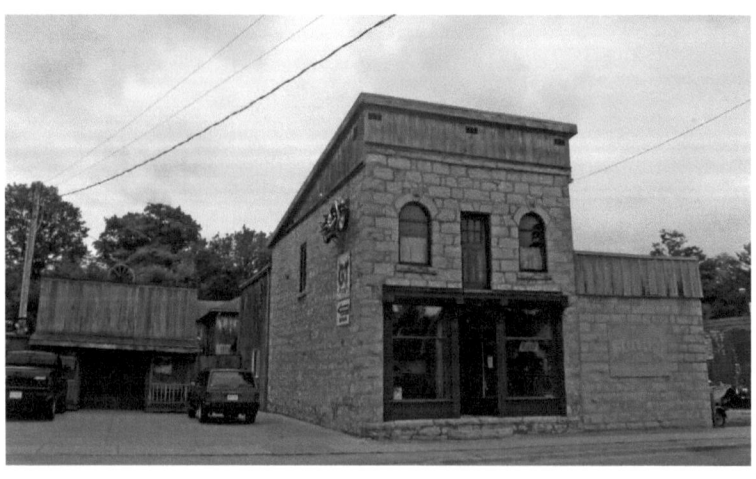

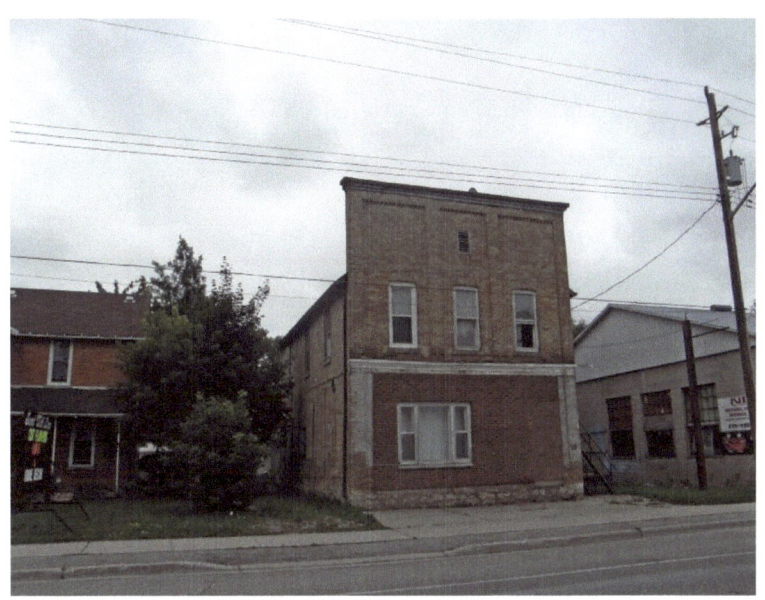

Yellow brick storefront

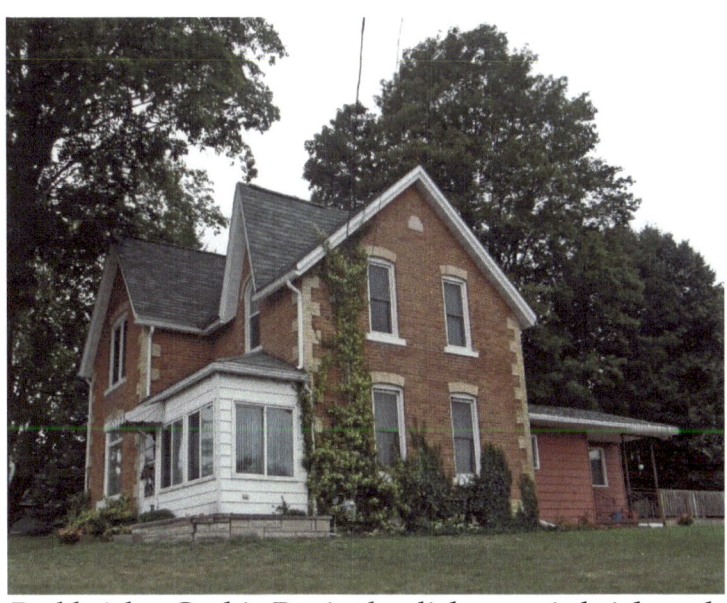

Red brick – Gothic Revival – dichromatic brickwork

Belvedere: (from the Italian "beautiful view") an architectural feature on a roof, in a garden or on a terrace that gives a beautiful view. Example: Port Elgin, see Page 24	
Brackets: a decorative or weight-bearing structural element which forms a right angle with one side against a wall and the other under a projecting surface such as an eave or roof. Example: 536 Mill Street, Port Elgin, see Page 23	
Cobblestone architecture: Refers to the use of cobblestones embedded in mortar as a method for erecting walls on houses and commercial buildings. Example: Port Elgin, see Page 22	
Cornice: originally the wooden overhang of the roof. With the use of stone, brick, iron and steel, the cornice is any projecting shelf at the top of a ceiling or roof. They can be very decorative. Example: 559 Mill Street, Port Elgin, Page 21	
Dentil Moulding: an even series of rectangles used as ornamental decoration in cornices. Example:	
Dormer: (French for "sleep") a gable end window that pierces through the plane of a sloping roof surface to create usable space in the top floor or attic of a building by adding headroom. Example: 559 Mill Street, Port Elgin, Page 22	

Finial: ornament added to the top of a gable, pinnacle, canopy or spire – a Gothic element. Example of Finial: Port Elgin, see Page 34	
Fretwork: interlaced decorative design resembling a bracket. Example: Port Elgin, see Page 25	
Frontispiece: a portion of the façade of a building, usually a centred doorway, that is slightly raised from the rest of the building, usually has extensive ornamentation. Frontispieces are usually Classical in design with white columned porches. Example: Port Elgin library, see Page 33	
Gable: the triangular portion of a wall between the edges of a sloping roof. Example: Shallow Lake, see Page 60	
Hipped Roof: a roof where all sides slope downwards to the walls with no gables. Example: Port Elgin, see Page 41	
Keystones and Voussoirs: a voussoir is a wedge-shaped element used in building an arch. A keystone is the central stone that locks all the stones into position, allowing the arch to bear weight. A keystone is often enlarged and embellished. Example: 490 Green Street, Port Elgin, see Page 17	

Lancet Window: a tall, narrow window with a pointed arch at its top. Example: 516 Mill Street, Port Elgin, Page 20	
Mansard Roof: This style was popularized by Francois Mansart (1598-1666), an accomplished architect of the French Baroque period and especially fashionable during the Second French Empire (1852-1870). This roof is almost flat on the top section, with two slopes on each of its sides with the lower slope at a steeper angle than the upper and having dormer windows. Example: Shallow Lake, see Page 64	
Pediment: a triangular section above the horizontal structure (entablature), typically supported by columns. The inside of the triangle is called the tympanum. Example: Port Elgin Public Library, Page 33	
Quoin: masonry blocks at the corner of a wall, often a decorative feature, usually larger or of a different colour than the rest of the wall. Example: 543 Mill Street, Port Elgin, Page 21	
Verge boards: also called bargeboards – hang from the projecting end of a roof and are often elaborately carved and ornamented. Example: Port Elgin, see Page 11	
Window Hood: A **hood** is the piece found above window openings, usually of an ornate design, and covers the top third of the opening. Hoods are commonly placed above arched or curved openings on both windows and doors. Example: 481 Elgin Street, Port Elgin, Page 42	

Port Elgin's Building Styles

Beaux Arts: Many of the Beaux Arts buildings were banks, post offices, and railway stations. The Ontario Beaux Arts style is eclectic mixing elements of Classical, Renaissance and Baroque. Often the designs have a temple-like façade, pedimented porticos, balustrades, capitals in many styles. Example: Public Library, Port Elgin, Page 33	
Regency Cottage, 1830-1860 – This style originated in England in 1815 and spread to Ontario later in the 19th century as British officers retired to Canada. It is a modest one-storey house with a low-pitched hip roof and has a symmetrical front façade. Example: see Page 41, Port Elgin	
Gothic Revival, 1830-1890 – These decorative buildings have sharply-pitched gables with highly detailed verge boards, pointed-arch window openings, and dichromatic brickwork. It is a common style in Ontario. Example: 464 Mill Street, Port Elgin, Page 18	
Italianate, 1850-1900 – It has wide-bracketed eaves, belvederes, wrap-around verandahs. Example: 559 Mill Street, Port Elgin, Page 22	
Queen Anne, 1885-1900 – This style is distinguished by an irregular outline featuring a combination of an offset tower, broad gables, projecting two-storey bays, verandahs, multi-sloped roofs, and tall, decorative chimneys. A mixture of brick and wood is common. Example: 543 Mill Street, Port Elgin, Page 21	

www.ingramcontent.com/pod-product-compliance
Lightning Source LLC
Chambersburg PA
CBHW040811200526
45159CB00022B/260